MAGICIAN

The Lost Journals of the Magus
Geoffrey Carlyle

MAGICIAN

The Lost Journals of the Magus
Geoffrey Carlyle

Edited by
Robert Holdstock & Malcolm Edwards

Illustrated by Dan Woods

Paper Tiger

A Dragon's World Ltd Imprint

Dragon's World Ltd
Limpsfield
SURREY RH8 0DY
Great Britain

Design and Art Direction by Steve Henderson
Plans sketched by David Heal

Hardback: ISBN 905895 70 3
Limpback: ISBN 905895 69 X

Printed in Hong Kong

CONTENTS

INTRODUCTION

In the late spring of 1977 renovation and repair work was begun on Ruckhurst Manor, a Tudor house hidden amid a stand of oak forest on the Wiltshire Downs. Neglected by its last owner, the house had stood empty, and increasingly derelict, for nearly 35 years. It was in an advanced state of dilapidation, and substantial reconstruction was needed in order to make it habitable.

It was during inspection work in the East cellar that the astonishing nature of the house and its site was discovered. The flagstones of the passage leading to the cellar were found to form the roof of an underground tunnel; this led into a wide, low-ceilinged chamber formed partly from stone slabs and partly from an ancient excavation into the natural Wiltshire sandstone.

Sealed for four centuries, the chamber contained the equipment and manuscripts of a medieval alchemist and magus – a practitioner of what is commonly termed black magic. It is these writings that form the subject of this book.

At first sight Ruckhurst Manor is a traditional early 16th century country house, with 14 rooms, servants' quarters, and an estate of 45 acres, mostly oak woodland. The house is known to students of ghosts and hauntings, because in the 17th and 18th centuries it was renowned as one of the most haunted houses in England. The recent discoveries at Ruckhurst provide a possible, though remarkable, explanation for its history.

In the early part of the 17th century the cellars were reportedly exorcised by the Bishop of Gloucester at the behest of the Gilpin family, to whom ownership had passed in 1611. They continued to be troubled by strange noises and apparitions and a further exorcism was undertaken, but apparently to no avail. The Gilpins left the house to take up residence in Salisbury and Ruckhurst's history becomes obscure for 40 years, until it came into the possession of the Cromwells. It seems that they too had problems, for there is a long-standing (though unsubstantiated) local tradition that Oliver himself once came to stay at the house, but departed in considerable haste after a single night; the stories suggest that the ghost of Charles I appeared in his room.

Eighty years later the German ghost-hunter Hans Kruppen wrote, after visiting the house, of a 'nightmare encounter' with an apparition so terrifying that he refused to describe it in his otherwise exhaustive memoirs. In 1787 the celebrated

Scottish psychic Mary Forsythe reported sensing at Ruckhurst a 'residuum of fear that so permeates the house it becomes tangible in every shadow, in every flicker of candle flame'.

Ruckhurst Manor was by this time notorious, and for several years remained uninhabited. However, towards the end of the 18th century the hauntings appear to have ceased, or at least subsided considerably, for the house was then bought by the Higham family of Marlborough, in 1796, and they lived there for more than a century without apparently being troubled by any sort of 'nightmare encounter'. The house was visited in the 1930s by the famous ghost-hunter Harry Price, who reported it devoid of any unusual aspects. It has subsequently become no more than a minor footnote in the copious modern literature of haunted buildings.

The manor house itself has only been cosmetically extended since its erection in 1524, but the building at that time made extensive use of stone from an earlier structure, a smaller late 14th century lodge known as Hartshurst. Parts of that building remain in the ground plan and the cellar, for reasons which are now obvious.

The earliest reference to any building on the site may be in the *Domesday Book*: 'An unfarmed hold of thirty hides, at Hartehurst, with hall and barns. Put out for punishment as witches and Henry Lachard installed to return to crop.' Excavation around the periphery of the house has now shown that the site was inhabited from about 3000 BC. Since Ruckhurst Manor stands on a natural mound its advantage as a defensible site can be readily understood.

The size of the mound was increased in Neolithic times by the building of a stone-lined burial chamber, reached by a spiral passageway; it is this chamber which formed the basis of the magus's hidden workplace (see below).

The community that built this tomb also lived upon the mound and continued to do so until they were ejected, or taken over, by the invading Beaker folk, the first of the Bronze Age peoples to enter the area. The Beaker habitation blends almost smoothly with the next settlement, that of the Belgic peoples of the early Iron Age. This Celtic tribe extended the holding, building their palisade further down the mound, and constructing perhaps ten houses inside. Evidence from the excavation suggests that the arrival of the Iron Age peoples had little substantial effect on the occupants of the mound, but rather that they integrated with the mound dwellers.

The occupation was broken in Romano-British times, but from approximately the 7th century AD onwards the rise of ground was occupied by a Saxon hall, with associated outhouses; this was the Hartehurst referred to in the *Domesday Book*. It stayed substantially intact until being replaced by a stone and wood building in about 1370.

No other occupation in pre-Roman times was ever quite as smooth as the occupation of Ruckhurst mound seems to have been. Even then the site appears to have had some religious or mystical significance sufficiently important to transcend the cultural and other differences of the several races. The exact nature of that significance is unclear, but the best evidence comes not from the excavation work, but from the remarkable manuscripts of the magus, Geoffrey Carlyle.

Geoffrey Carlyle, (1496–1571?), was an alchemist and occultist of some repute who is known from the *Victoria County History of Wiltshire* to have been resident at the house as early as 1518, and to have been its sole owner from 1520, at which time he initiated the work of replacing the 14th century building with the new and enlarged house which he renamed Ruckhurst Manor. Carlyle's origins are obscure, but a son Geoffrey is recorded as having been christened in Oxted in 1498, born to Edwin and Elizabeth Carlyle of that parish. That son is recorded as having disappeared in 1508, and although there is a ten year gap between that date and his first recorded appearance at Hartshurst (as it then was), there is every reason to suppose, given the evidence in Carlyle's manuscript, that the two Geoffreys are one and the same, and that the boy was 'stolen' from his parents for some occult purpose at the behest of Hartshurst's owner, James Crooke.

Crooke was himself an alchemist of minor note, and in 1508 — the year of Geoffrey's disappearance from Oxted — was host to the celebrated European occultist Cornelius Agrippa von Nettesheim (only twenty-two at the time of his visit). Both men were eminently respectable, at least outwardly, but one idea which surfaces repeatedly in Carlyle's manuscript is that *genuine* masters of the secret arts — as opposed to the many charlatans who have gained publicity over the centuries — maintained at all times an unimpeachable reputation in the community at large, while practising in conditions of utmost secrecy. It is possible to surmise that the boy's abduction and Agrippa's visit may well have been connected, and indeed that the boy may have been intended as a sacrifice in some ritual. (Carlyle's notes describe confinement in the hidden room below the house — 'learned early of the agonies of abstinence, forced upon me in the chamber below the flags where the stone absorbed my screams', he writes — so it is clear that, at least initially, he was a prisoner.) We can only guess at what saved him; perhaps Agrippa noticed some potential in the boy. Whatever the reason, Carlyle seems to have followed Agrippa back to Europe and spent several years training with him, before returning to England in 1518.

Two years later, in 1520, an event which now seems to have sinister significance occurred. In his manuscript Carlyle refers only in passing to the deaths of Crooke and his wife, but a contemporary account may be found in a letter written to Henry VIII by Edward Cecil, a friend of the Crookes and a Wiltshire landowner. The letter includes the following description of their deaths: 'In truth, my lord, they were much agonized, even a week before their death appearing pallid and pocked, their eyes widened by tormenting visions and terrifying fancies. Crooke spoke of bursts of fire from his limbs, that burned but left no mark. Lady Mary complained of hands at her throat, day and night. In this manner, strangled and burned, I was to witness their sad corpses this last October. The man Geoffrey is himself severely palsied, his skin covered in rashes, and he is subject to periods of great fatigue.'

No suspicion focused on Carlyle — death from painful disease was commonplace enough in the 16th century — but reading his manuscripts raises the strong possibility (if we assume the truth of their contents) that he brought about the Crookes' deaths by occult means. He frequently refers to the great tiredness, even paralysis, which overtakes a magus at the end of a difficult or dangerous conjuration, and the similarity between his descriptions and his condition as recorded in Cecil's letter seems too great to be coincidental.

For some years after he inherited the house Carlyle was a virtual recluse. Ostensibly he was engaged in building Ruckhurst Manor, but from his journals it is clear that for the most part he spent these years enlarging the ancient tomb below the east cellar, and equipping it most thoroughly as a laboratory for alchemical and occult studies.

When records and letters mention him again, it is as an eminent and generous — if somewhat aloof — member of the community, and a man who moved easily in court circles. He was known chiefly as an alchemical scholar and researcher, and also practised such minor occult arts as astrology and physiognomy. He was also a member of Agrippa's Brothers of the Golden Cross, but of greater interest is his participation in a secret brotherhood that Carlyle refers to in his journal as the Enneas.

We can only guess at the nature of the Enneas. The name suggests nine members, and it appears that they were an all-powerful secret society of practising mages. No other record of this body has been traced, so its origin and history remain obscure. We do not know how long it endured after Carlyle's death; indeed, it is not impossible that it still exists today.

Members of the Enneas all had secret names known only to each other. Carlyle's cognomen was Rofocale Meister (Master of Lucifuge Rofocale), or Rofomagus. This alone indicates his extraordinary eminence in the ranks of his fellow magicians, for Lucifuge Rofocale is one of the chief ministers of the Descending Hierarchy of Hell, and although it is possible for a magician to conclude a pact with him, *mastery* is — or should be — impossible.

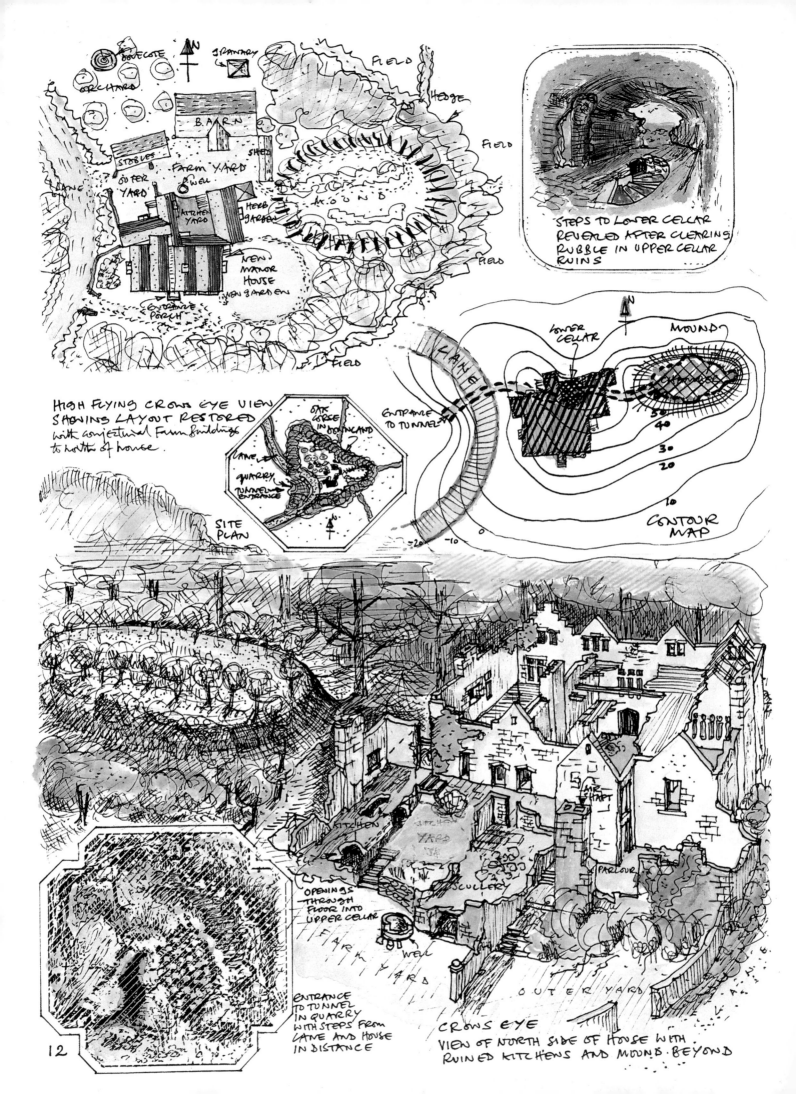

DOVECOTE

ORCHARD

N

GRANARY

B·A·R·N

STABLES

SHED

FARM YARD

OUTER YARD

WELL

KITCHEN YARD

HERB GARDEN

NEW MANOR HOUSE

NEW GARDEN

ENTRANCE PORCH

LANE

FIELD

HEDGE

FIELD

MOUND

FIELD

FIELD

STEPS TO LOWER CELLAR REVEALED AFTER CLEARING RUBBLE IN UPPER CELLAR RUINS

HIGH FLYING CROWS EYE VIEW SHOWING LAYOUT RESTORED with conjectural Farm Buildings to North of house.

OAK COPSE IN DOWN LAND

LANE

QUARRY

TUNNEL ENTRANCE

SITE PLAN

ENTRANCE TO TUNNEL

LANE

LOWER CELLAR

MOUND

N

50
40
30
20
10
0
-20 -10

CONTOUR MAP

OPENINGS THROUGH FLOOR INTO UPPER CELLAR

KITCHEN

KITCHEN YARD

AIR SHAFT

PARLOUR

SCULLERY

F A R M Y A R D

WELL

O U T E R Y A R D

ENTRANCE TO TUNNEL IN QUARRY WITH STEPS FROM LANE AND HOUSE IN DISTANCE

CROWS EYE
VIEW OF NORTH SIDE OF HOUSE WITH RUINED KITCHENS AND MOUND BEYOND

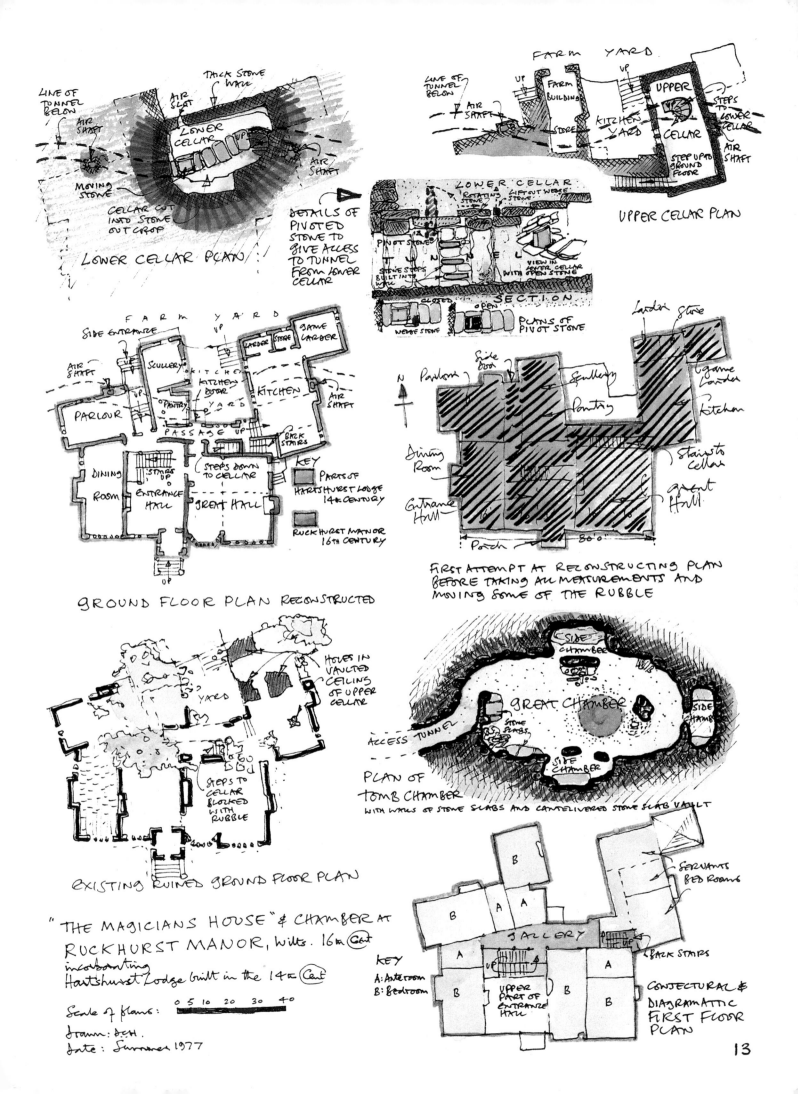

LINE OF TUNNEL BELOW

AIR SLOT

THICK STONE WALL

AIR SHAFT

LOWER CELLAR

UP

MOVING STONE

CELLAR CUT INTO STONE OUTCROP

AIR SHAFT

LOWER CELLAR PLAN

DETAILS OF PIVOTED STONE TO GIVE ACCESS TO TUNNEL FROM LOWER CELLAR

LOWER CELLAR

ROTATING STONE

LIFT OUT WEDGE STONE

PIVOT STONE

STONE STEPS BUILT INTO WALL

TUNNEL

VIEW IN LOWER CELLAR WITH OPEN STONE

CLOSED

OPEN

SECTION

WEDGE STONE

PLANS OF PIVOT STONE

FARM YARD

LINE OF TUNNEL BELOW

AIR SHAFT

UP

FARM BUILDING

STORE

UP

KITCHEN YARD

UPPER CELLAR

STEPS TO LOWER CELLAR

STEP UP TO GROUND FLOOR

AIR SHAFT

UPPER CELLAR PLAN

FARM YARD

SIDE ENTRANCE

UP

LARDER STORE GAME LARDER

AIR SHAFT

SCULLERY

KITCHEN

UP

KITCHEN PASSAGE

PANTRY

YARD

KITCHEN

AIR SHAFT

PARLOUR

PASSAGE UP

BACK STAIRS

DINING ROOM

STAIRS UP

ENTRANCE HALL

STEPS DOWN TO CELLAR

GREAT HALL

UP

KEY

PARTS OF HARTSHURST LODGE 14th CENTURY

RUCKHURST MANOR 16th CENTURY

GROUND FLOOR PLAN RECONSTRUCTED

N

Parlour

Side door

Scullery

Game Larder

Dining Room

Pantry

Kitchen

Entrance Hall

Stairs to Cellar

16'0"

Porch

80'0"

Great Hall

FIRST ATTEMPT AT RECONSTRUCTING PLAN BEFORE TAKING ALL MEASUREMENTS AND MOVING SOME OF THE RUBBLE

YARD

HOLES IN VAULTED CEILINGS OF UPPER CELLAR

STEPS TO CELLAR BLOCKED WITH RUBBLE

EXISTING RUINED GROUND FLOOR PLAN

SIDE CHAMBER

GREAT CHAMBER

ACCESS TUNNEL

STONE SLABS

SIDE CHAMBER

SIDE CHAMBER

PLAN OF TOMB CHAMBER

WITH WALLS OF STONE SLABS AND CANTILEVERED STONE SLAB VAULT

"THE MAGICIANS HOUSE" & CHAMBER AT RUCKHURST MANOR, Wilts. 16th Cent

incorporating

Hartshurst Lodge built in the 14th Cent

Scale of plans: 0 5 10 20 30 40

Drawn: BCH.

Date: Summer 1977

B

B

A A

SERVANTS BEDROOMS

B

GALLERY

A

UP

BACK STAIRS

KEY

A: ANTEROOM

B: BEDROOM

B

UPPER PART OF ENTRANCE HALL

A

B

CONJECTURAL & DIAGRAMMATIC FIRST FLOOR PLAN

13

If James Crooke was also a magician, then it is clear that he did not use the chamber below his house for his own purposes (although it seems evident that he knew of its existence), for the literature of magic is specific that only one magician may practise his art in a given place. If Carlyle did indeed cause the deaths of Crooke and his wife, a strong motive may have been to gain possession of the site, for the underground tomb made an ideal setting for his grisly research — completely hidden and unknown to any outsider. (Another motive may have been to gain admittance to the Enneas, for the name implies a fixed membership.) Whatever the motive, the murders show him to have been a single-minded and unsentimental character.

Access to the chamber was gained by lifting a flagstone in the cellar passage. From there to the chamber is a distance of forty feet along the spiralling tunnel — an uncomfortable journey, as the tunnel is only four feet high and less than two feet across. The main tomb chamber is fourteen feet high, with a base area of eighty square feet. There are four side chambers, in which the remains of the dead would originally have been placed. As such it is not only the largest known example of a tomb dating from the Megalithic Tomb Builder culture (which flourished in Ireland, Spain and the Mediterranean between five and six thousand years ago), but is also the only known example of this culture constructing such a tomb in England.

The passageway is lined by by uprights weighing, on average, two tons. The tomb chamber is lined by several rows of heavy blocks, and the vault is constructed of cunningly overlapped flagstones that allow it to rise to its full height. The vault is boulder capped, and the whole structure rises below the level ground that was the medieval kitchen garden, twenty yards from the house.

Carlyle evidently opened the rear wall of the chamber and discovered a small rock-hewn passage, filled with bones and stone tools. This area he extended — by what means we can only surmise, but significantly no trace of rubble from the excavation has been found — to create a cavern forty feet long, fifteen feet wide and rising to a height of ten feet. It was in this area that his workbench, scattered tools and equipment, and preserved parchments were found. Some faint traces of the pentagram used in his conjuration of demons could still be observed on the floor of the Neolithic tomb area, but the entire eastern end of the chamber appears to have been the scene of an intense conflagration. Carbon dating of fragments of feline remains found within the pentagram put the date of this fire at between 1550 and 1600.

The presentation of information in the manuscripts is untidy and chaotic, and perhaps reflects Carlyle's own uncertainty of the wisdom of what he was doing. They are essentially made up of three sections: first an account of Carlyle's life — his training as a magician, his researches and discoveries, and his attempts to outstrip any of his contemporaries or predecessors in his mastery of demons, and thus in his ability to perform magic. (These efforts seem eventually, as we shall see, to have led to his downfall.) Secondly there is a partial history of magic, as revealed by his enquiries, viewing the past through his control of the demon Astaroth. Thirdly, there are details of spells he employed: the preparations, the manner of the conjuration, and observations on the results. His subject is unorthodox, but Carlyle clearly had the scientist's instinct for the analysis and recording of results. There are hints in the manuscripts that it was his eventual intention to reorder all the material; the result would then have been a comprehensive manual of magic, worth all the corrupt and incomplete grimoires known to exist put together. As it is, Carlyle's manuscripts offer glimpses into a world of occult practice far beyond anything hitherto known.

The fragmentary nature of the manuscripts is exacerbated by Carlyle's use of misdirections and codes. Some are simple confusions, designed to mislead anyone who should by mischance stumble across the manuscript — intentionally misplaced phrases, mirror writing, ambiguities. More problematical are the codes. One is a transposition code, variable but decipherable; the other is very possibly not a code at all, but some invented or rediscovered ancient language, unrelated to any known tongue. Repetitive, gruff and guttural, it has thus far resisted analysis.

In the presentation here of extracts from Carlyle's manuscripts we have attempted two things:

first, to give as broad a flavour as possible of the variable content; secondly, to provide visual reconstruction of many of the scenes and visions mentioned, where possible following the indications of Carlyle's own sketches. A number of manuscript fragments are included, so that readers may appreciate the difficult nature of the original. In presenting translated extracts we have where possible clarified the antiquated language, without losing the subtle sense of his meaning. For reasons which should be obvious we have stopped short of giving the complete information which would enable others to try to emulate Carlyle. Excavation at the site (whose precise location must remain hidden) and analysis of the manuscripts are likely to continue for many years.

What are we to make, ultimately, of these remarkable manuscripts? Are they the fanciful imaginings of a medieval alchemist who liked to suppose that he was something more? Or are they, as the evidence surrounding their discovery suggests, a great deal more significant? If they are authentic records of a practising medieval magician — records which should never have been seen by unauthorized eyes but through fortuitous circumstances have survived four hundred years to be uncovered — then they add enormously to our knowledge of occult practices. Time will provide an answer to the question; but whatever that answer may be, the manuscripts remain a fascinating and enigmatic glimpse of the life of a man dedicated to the pursuit of power — Rofocale Meister. Rofomagus.

CHAPTER ONE
APPRENTICESHIP

These are the names by which I am known:
I am Geoffrey Carlyle, the name I acquired by accident — which is to say, my birth, over which I exerted no control. Thus am I known outside the Enneas, where my fame as alchemist, occultist and scholar is small but respectable.

I am also Rofocale Meister, which is to say *Rofomagus!* This is my true identity, and the name by which I am known to others of the inner fraternity, and to those spirits and demons whose actions I am able to control. He who reads this work should tremble at that name, for its meaning is clear and awesome. I am master of the great Prince Lucifuge Rofocale, Prime Minister of Hell. None other has such mastery.

And I am a name yet unwritten, for my endeavour is not complete. As I break the rule of writing, so shall I break the law of summoning, and aquire a new and more terrible name as evidence of a further mas tery, accomplishment of which has hitherto been supposed impossible

Introduction to the Ruckhurst Manuscript

Training

The opening section of Carlyle's manuscript is the one which comes closest to straightforward autobiography, and much of this is too mundane to be of interest here, though as an account of early 16th century domestic life it is certainly of historical value. There are passing references to Crooke's occult skills, and to Carlyle's earliest training in these areas, but nothing is discussed in detail until he begins to record his apprenticeship to Agrippa von Nettesheim.

Henry Cornelius Agrippa von Nettesheim (1486–1535) was the most important occultist of his time; his major work, the *Occult Philosophy*, remains a classic statement of the philosophy and science of magic. That it only encompassed a small part of Agrippa's knowledge becomes evident, however, from Carlyle's account.

I travelled with Agrippa to Paris where, under his tutelage, I began my education in earnest. We dwelt in a small house with a cellar which he consecrated for his operations; it had previously been a place where wine was stored, and no matter how many fumigations were performed, or braziers burned, a pervasive vinous odour filled it afterwards. It was in this dim and damp room that I witnessed for the first time the summoning of a demon, which sight filled me at once with fear, with awe, and with elation. The latter emotion was the strongest, for already I embraced my destiny most powerfully.

The name of the Prince summoned that time by Agrippa was Glasyalabolas, a most learned figure who I was to see often in the years that followed. The purpose of this summoning was primarily one of demonstration, so Agrippa merely instructed Glasyalabolas to enunciate certain mathematical theorems, which he did without apparent demur. At the time I understood little of what was said, and stood as if transfixed in the circle marked out for me, sensible of Agrippa's admonition not to move unless I wished to lose my soul. Agrippa seemed satisfied by what passed between the demon and himself, and shortly dismissed him.

When the ceremony was over and Agrippa turned to me, I observed with surprise the sudden pallor of his complexion, and the lines which had appeared on his brow. Instructing me on divers menial tasks to be performed, he adjourned to his chamber at the top of the house and did not reappear for three days, by which time he had regained his normal healthy mien. Thus I saw for the first time the strain placed upon the magus's mind and body by even the most familiar conjuration, an effect which may be likened to the constant performance of strenuous labour over a period of several days without sleep. Those impostors who claim to perform magical operations with simple incantations and much waving of staffs understand little of what is required.

In the years that followed, my education progressed under Agrippa's guidance. He was truly the greatest Master of the Arts; no other could have taught so much. I had instruction in every area of knowledge: in philosophy, in the sciences, in mathematics, in history, in languages, and much else. Members of the Enneas, and all true practitioners of magic, extend as far as possible their mastery of all of them. Much of this tuition took place in an upstairs room which Agrippa had made into a classroom; here, under his impatient eye, I laboured for weeks and months without end. Sometimes I would be taught by demons summoned by Agrippa for this purpose, for many of these Princes, though fallen, are most learned, and their teaching is without peer for their knowledge is infallible. Glasyalabolas was one such, with mastery over all arts and sciences. I stood within a circle at a lectern receiving instruction while Agrippa, having bound the demon securely into its circle with a spell of great potency, left us in order to continue his own studies. In due course my learning would have made me a prized scholar at any university in Europe.

My occult education proceeded simultaneously, much of it also imparted in the classroom. There was also much practical knowledge to be gained, and for this Agrippa and I journeyed far out of Paris, often at night. I learned of the many herbs and plants used in magic, and the incantations and precautions which must accompany their plucking; I stood at Agrippa's side as he practised necromancy in the graveyard of a tiny church on the outskirts of Paris; I learned to see and to control the elementals of earth and air, fire and water; I became expert in the skills of the blacksmith, the carpenter and the glassblower, in order that I might manufacture my own instruments of the art.

In time I was ready to attempt my own first spell. Agrippa had instructed me in a simple form of incantation which would restore life to a dead lizard. Under his watchful eye I compounded a paste of sulphur, the ground bones of a frog, virgin earth and divers herbs, applied it to the animal's skin with a fine brush of corpse hair, and spoke the words of the incantation as the room filled with incense from the brazier I had lit. As I concluded the ritual so the lizard stirred; its legs twitched; its eyes moved; then it was still once more. Afterwards Agrippa scolded me severely over my carelessness in several aspects of the preparation, which had diluted the spell's potency, but I was nonetheless elated, for the creature *had* moved. Mastery, I knew even then, would follow with practice.

Thus it proved. Within the year I could perform such simple operations with ease, and was ready for more advanced work. Agrippa admitted my aptitude as a pupil. I sent forth a minor hurt to plague a nobleman who had displeased Agrippa at court; I compounded a most efficacious love spell; by the end of my fourth year with Agrippa I was fit to attempt the summoning of a demon.

At this point the manuscript breaks into the undeciphered code which recurs elsewhere at intervals, evidently when Carlyle felt it wise to conceal the details of an operation. This seems primarily to have been his practice in the earliest of his writings, for those of later years give such details far more openly. It seems that he was at first worried lest his writings find their way into other hands, but that this fear subsided with time.

Equipment

Carlyle's journals contain a great deal of detailed information on the preparation of the various tools and instruments of magic, and on the purification of the magus himself prior to embarking on any conjuration. These reflect the instructions to be found in the most authoritative grimoires, where great stress is laid on the need for consecration and purification of everything used in a magical operation. The incantations which accompany these preparations are extremely lengthy and repetitive, and great importance is given to the requirement that they be followed with absolute fidelity, no matter how pointless or absurd they may seem. These incantations have been omitted. In the extracts which follow he describes the various equipment required by the magus.

The Garments To Be Worn By The Magus: A simple gown is to be worn, adorned only with these symbols:

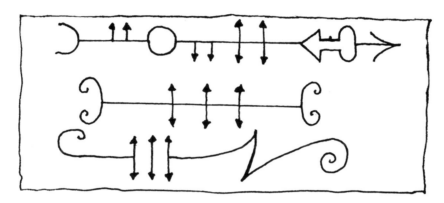

The gown is to be woven of silk; or, if this be unavailable, of linen. If linen is to be used, the thread must have been spun by a young maiden of proven chastity. In certain operations a belt made from the skin of a lion may be worn. The shoes are of white leather, and must be made during the nine days preceding an operation. The crown, if it be worn, is of virgin parchment, and written on it are these names: to the fore, YOD HE VAU HE; to the right, EL; to the left, ELOHIM; to the rear, ADONAI. These names are to be written using the ink and pen of the art.

The Instruments of the Art: These are the instruments required by the operator: the knife with a black hilt; the knife with a white hilt; the scimitar; the sickle; the dagger; the poniard; the short lance; the staff; the wand; the sword; the further swords for the use of assistants; the burin. Each is to be made in the prescribed manner, as follows:

The knife with the white hilt may be used in all operations save only the making of the circle. It is to be made in the day and the hour of Mercury, the Moon being full, and must be dipped in a mixture of pimpernel juice and the blood of a gosling, and inscribed with the necessary characters. The knife with the black hilt, which is used in making the circle, is to be made in the day and the hour of Saturn, and dipped in a mixture of hemlock juice and the blood of a black cat.

(There follow similar instructions for the preparation of the other metal instruments. The 'making of the circle' referred to here is the symbolic tracing, with the black-handled knife, of the circles, pentagrams and symbols within whose protection the magus may summon a demon.)

The staff is to be of elderwood or rosewood, and the wand of hazel. They must be cut from the tree at sunrise on the day of Mercury, and inscribed in that day and hour. The wood must be virgin: new branches of a year's growth, no more. Once prepared they should be consecrated and set aside in a place of purity until they are required.

All instruments of the art must be prepared and consecrated in the nine days preceding the operation, and then must be wrapped in silk of any colour save black or grey. The silk must previously have been incensed and consecrated, and set aside for seven days among sweet spices.

The Pen and the Parchment: The pen is to be made from the feather of a male gosling: the magus must pluck the third feather of the right wing, meanwhile speaking this incantation: 'ADRAI, HAHLII, TAMAII, TILONAS, ATHAMAS, ZIANOR, ADONAI banish from this pen all deceit and error, so that it may be of virtue and efficacy to write all that I desire'. It should then be sharpened with the knife of the art, perfumed and sprinkled, and set aside in a silk cloth.

The incantation must be written, using the pen of the art, on virgin parchment: that is, parchment taken from an animal which has not attained the age of procreation. This animal, which must be male, should be taken by the magus in the day and hour of Mercury to a secret place, where no one may see him at work. He must carry with him a marsh reed, cut with a single stroke by a new knife, and before commencing must strip the leaves from it, meanwhile repeating the Conjuration of the Reed. This having been spoken, the animal may be flayed, and the skin rubbed with exorcised salt. It must then be left in the sun for a day, after which it is placed in a glazed vessel filled with lime and exorcised water, and left for three days, then scraped, stretched on a circle of hazel, then dried for three days in a dark place. The cauls of new-born children may also be employed for this purpose.

The candles are to be made in the day of Mercury from virgin wax: that is, wax made by bees which have not made wax previously. This wax must be gathered by the magus himself. The wicks are to be made by the magus, or by a young virgin.

The Preparation of the Magus: In the nine days preceding any operation, the magus must prepare himself in the proper manner, having first made ready the necessary instruments. He must bathe in exorcised water, and purify himself thereby from the crown of his head to his toe, and after speaking the necessary prayer should dry himself with a towel of white linen, and dress in the gown of white linen or silk. Henceforth until the time of the operation he must abstain from all things unlawful, and from every kind of impiety, impurity, wickedness or immodesty of body or soul. He must abstain from excessive eating or drinking, and from useless conversation, and must observe a strict decency in all things. It is best if he remains solitary during this time, seeing and speaking to no one save any assistants he may employ, and fasting as much as he is able.

Grimoires

Carlyle devotes considerable space to the discussion of a number of grimoires and their use. All are known to modern occultists and researchers, with the exception of the work he calls the *Nygromancyene*, which was his own grimoire. This, it may be presumed, was lost in the accident which consumed Carlyle and much of his workshop. The surviving journals and fragments present a tantalizing glimpse of the knowledge which must have been contained within the pages of that work. What follows is an abbreviated version of his writing on grimoires:

I have devoted many months to the acquisition and study of the several grimoires purporting to give instruction on the summoning of demons, and have contemplated the composition of a treatise examining each in detail and assessing their efficacy. This work must await a time of greater leisure. The value of these books varies greatly; some are evidently the work of charlatans, others are useful and accurate guides, though in almost every case deficient in some particular. Foremost among the works of fakery is a book of recent origin known as the *Black Pullet*, which has nonetheless acquired a certain notoriety. Its suggestion that a Prince of Hell may be summoned by the simple expedient of cleaving in twain a black hen at a crossroads at midnight while repeating a simple incantation reveals that the author, whoever he may be, has no knowledge of the rigours of true magic.

The works which were most frequently used in my own instruction, and which I have ever found of value, are the *Clavicula Salomnis* and the *Legemeton*, the so-called Lesser Key of Solomon (though my scrying of the past leads me to the certain conclusion that the attribution of both books to King Solomon is false). Whereas the Key itself is of great philosophical value to the magus, the *Legemeton* is of greater practical use in its detailed description of the steps to be taken in performing a summoning. I have greatly amended and refined the knowledge contained in both books in the course of my own studies.

Also of value is the *Book of Sacred Magic*, composed by the mage Abra-Melin, known also as Abraham the Jew. This work was composed by the great magician shortly before his death and passed to his son Lamech, whereafter a copy made by Lamech came into the possession of Agrippa. I composed a further

copy, and these three are the only versions in existence, to my knowledge. The original is now in the possession of Lamech's son, himself called Abraham, an elderly and ineffectual necromancer now resident in Zurich; Agrippa's copy disappeared after his death and may have been destroyed. I have spoken with Abra-Melin through the veils of time and found him a most learned scholar, though lacking the ambition to extend his powers to their fullest extent. His work has greatly facilitated my own.

I term my own grimoire the *Nygromancyene*, and within its pages is to be found knowledge exceeding that recorded in all other grimoires. Through careful study of the preparations and procedures recorded therein any apprentice magician might in a matter of years acquire the level of mastery over the Princes of the Descending Hierarchy which took me decades of slow research. In time I shall find a suitable apprentice to train in its use; though if I succeed in my ultimate ambitions this course of action may prove unnecessary.

Seals and Symbols

Symbolism of all kinds is central to the practice of magic, and Rofomagus records in detail many of the signs, seals and symbols which he employed. Each demon is represented by its own seal, which would be affixed to any pact reached with a magician as a binding commitment. The magician, too, would have *his* seal, whose form would symbolically represent him. Rofomagus's seal is reproduced on several occasions in his manuscript. Its exact significance inevitably eludes us; it is his magical signature, as unique to him as our ordinary signatures are to us. The signs most commonly used in his magic are the many Pentacles, or Medals, of which there are altogether 44, each with its particular characteristics and uses. A few selected examples are reproduced here:

The Pentacles may be used to strike terror into spirits, and to make them obedient. They are also efficacious against all perils of earth and air, fire and water; against poison which has been drunk; against all manner of infirmity; to protect against sorcery; and if armed with them the magus may proceed without fear in almost any circumstances.

The Pentacles may be drawn on exorcised virgin parchment, or inscribed in metal. The colour of ink or the metal used must be that appropriate to the Planet with which the Pentacle is in sympathy. These are as follows:

The Seven Pentacles of Saturn: black; lead
The Seven Pentacles of Jupiter: blue; tin
The Seven Pentacles of Mars: red; iron
The Seven Pentacles of the Sun: yellow; gold
The Five Pentacles of Venus: green; copper
The Five Pentacles of Mercury: mixed colours; a mixture of metals
The Six Pentacles of the Moon: silver; silver

The First Pentacle of Saturn is of great use in striking terror into the spirits. Upon being shown it they submit and kneel on the earth before the magus, and obey his command.

The Sixth Pentacle of Saturn is formed from the mystical characters of Saturn, and around it is written in Hebrew these words: 'Set thou a wicked one to be ruler over him, and let Satan stand at his right hand.' The person against whom the magus uses this Pentacle will be obsessed by demons, and shall ever fear their coming, and shall have no peace, and in sleep shall suffer dreadful nightmares, and shall eventually take his own life in despair unless the magus shall relent.

The Second Pentacle of Jupiter is greatly efficacious in the acquisition of riches and honours, and the user will enjoy great peace of mind. It may also be used to discover hidden treasures, and to drive away any guardian spirits. This Pentacle should be inscribed on virgin parchment with the blood of a screech owl, using a feather from a swallow's wing.

The Sixth Pentacle of Mars will protect the magus against any attacker, howsoever armed. He will not be injured in any way, and his assailant's weapons will be turned against himself. The words to be inscribed around the Pentacle are these: 'Their sword shall enter their own heart, and their bow shall be broken.'

The Fifth Pentacle of the Sun will summon those spirits who will transport the magus great distances in a short period of time, lifting him into the air but keeping him hidden from any watcher upon the ground.

The Fifth Pentacle of Venus will incite strong feelings of love and devotion in anyone to whom it is shown; its inscription, which should be recited aloud, is 'My heart is like wax, it is melted in the midst of my bowels.'

The Fourth Pentacle of Mercury is used in the acquisition of knowledge, and the seeking out of things that are hidden, and in the comprehension of mysteries. The spirits which it calls forth may be commanded to perform missions on the magus's behalf.

The Fifth Pentacle of Mercury commands the spirits of the planet, and causes any door to open, however securely it may be fastened.

The Second Pentacle of the Moon preserves the user against all perils and dangers associated with water, and should thus be used before undertaking any journey by river or by sea. The spirits of the moon which it calls forth are troublesome, and may cause great storms and tempests in order to terrify the magus. On being shown the Pentacle, and having the words on it spoken to them, they will cease their mischief.

The Fifth Pentacle of the Moon is of great power. By its use the magus may obtain, during his sleep, the answers to mysteries which may baffle him. It may be used to invoke a spirit who will cause great destruction, and protect the magus against any phantom of the night. It is said that dead souls may be recalled from Hell itself by use of this Pentacle, but I have not found this to be so.

Rofomagus's manuscript goes on to discuss the symbolic importance of such magical seals, quoting a significant passage from the *Clavicula Salomnis*:

> 'Thou shouldest take particular care if thou makest them on virgin parchment to use the proper colours; and if thou engravest them on metal, to do so in the manner taught thee; and so shalt thou have the satisfaction of seeing them produce the desired effect. But seeing that this Science is not a Science of argument and open reasoning, but that, on the contrary, it is entirely mysterious and occult, we should not argue and deliberate over these matters, and it is sufficient to believe firmly to enable us to bring into operation that which hath already been taught.'

This emphasises a crucial point regarding much of the material recorded in Rofomagus's writings and reproduced in this book. The purpose of a given symbol or incantation may be obscure; parts of rituals may seem superfluous. Nevertheless, they must be followed with great precision if results are to be obtained, and scepticism in the mind of the operator rules out the possibility of success. No one can be a magician who does not believe whole-heartedly in the precepts of the art.

As a sorcerer, Geoffrey Carlyle's main ambition would have been to gather power to himself, assure his luck and good fortune, and to increase his control over the forces of the supernatural. At all times it would be necessary to defend himself against demons, stray evil and the 'evil eye', and to this end Carlyle possessed numerous talismans, each designed to ward off a different evil influence. Often inscribed upon an iron dagger, or on virgin parchment, with representations of daggers, eyes and other obscure symbols, Rofocale Meister would not have dared summon even his familiars without his 'armoury' of personal defences.

One seal in particular is of interest, and clearly ties in with Carlyle's final summoning and awful demise. It shows the 'plan' of the Neolithic tomb in which he had built his laboratory, and clearly depicted in its cruciform shape is the symbol of Lucifuge Rofocale. That same symbol, much obscured, can still be seen, pecked into the stone of the eastern chamber of the tomb. Rofomagus records only one, slightly cryptic, comment on the subject:

My vision has shown me Lucifuge, summoned and quiesced by the magic of the dawn people. This is his place, and his key is buried here. Without protection he was summoned and he obeyed, and the power of nature and the words of power M'GIRACHICH UNCHIRIK C'THANOGH were enough. Now I am Rofocale Meister, and his power in this place to summon, to destroy, to locate and to know is the second greatest of all powers, and is mine alone.

Familiars

Familiars — that is, demon spirits who have taken the form of ordinary animals — have always been closely identified with the practice of witchcraft, but they can also play a role in more powerful magic. Many magical operations require the presence of assistants (or Tanists, as they are sometimes termed), though they rarely have any significant role to perform other than merely being present. Rofomagus evidently found it simpler to employ familiars instead, as his journals tell us:

When the grimoires call for assistants to participate in a ritual I have found it less troublesome to employ certain creatures which I have trained to the task. These I refer to as my familiars, though they are not the simple creatures of Hades which popular belief supposes the pets of witches to be. Unlike human assistants, their discretion is never in doubt.

The following
creatures are
best suited to the
role of familiar: the
cat, the owl, the raven,
the toad and the bat. A
male animal is to be used, and
should be operated upon in the
month of its birth so that it loses its
generative ability. A spell of simple
understanding, spoken over an animal
rendered insensible through inhalation of
laudanum, binds it to its master and en-
ables it to perform its simple task, as long as it
is kept in the proper state of preparedness. It
must be fed solely on human flesh and blood, on
which diet it will grow fat and torpid, and hostile to
anyone save its master. During the nine days preceding
a magical operation in which it is to participate the familiar
must fast, as a result of which it will become particularly
vicious. It must be controlled carefully at this time, for which a
few words of power, or the appropriate Pentacle, should suffice; if
it should bite or scratch the magus his preparations will be spoilt, and
the whole operation will have to be started again from the beginning.

When the time comes and the circles are drawn the familiar will go without prompting to its correct place, and it can be relied on never to stray during the ceremony. Whereas the human assistant may be deceived by an artful and cunning demon and tempted to his doom, the familiar, bound to the voice of the magus alone, is oblivious to such temptation.

After the operation is completed the familiar must be permitted to feed as much as it wishes, and then to sleep.

It has been my observation that a familiar enjoys a lifespan greatly in excess of that usually achieved by its species. One cat which served me well through many of my researches attained a span of nearly two-score years. Once a familiar dies it may be consumed by its fellows. This is the only permissible exception to their habitual diet.

Animal Creations

It is clear from his writings that Carlyle's instincts were those of the scientist, even though his researches were in areas far removed from what we think of as science. Occasionally his work did proceed on similar lines to experiments carried out in the ordinary (that is, non-occult) world, as is the case with his attempts to create animal hybrids.

The five years past I have been much exercised by the problems of creating, by techniques both secular and magical, new and hybrid forms from different existing species of bird, beast and reptile.

    My interest in this new form of knowledge was aroused while I was still under Agrippa's tutelage, when I was introduced to the sketches and notes of the remarkable Italian scholar Leonardo, who attempted by cunning surgery to amalgamate forms as a botanist does, grafting parts of one creature on to the body of another. His ingenuity was great, but his efforts were thwarted through his ignorance of the thaumaturgic techniques which must be employed if flesh is to be married to other, unfamiliar flesh. No other magus has embarked upon such an endeavour, seeing no profit in it other than in the production of freaks for display at travelling fairs, so it proved necessary for me to develop all the necessary techniques.

Firstly I summoned the demon Sothyrmes. He is a minor Prince, not difficult to control and learned in matters of anatomy, but withal capricious, mischievous and unreliable. It required all my command to bring forth from him answers which were neither incomplete nor misleading. By dint of much perseverance I learned that the type of suture to be employed depends on the nature of the hybrid: to join mammal to reptile or bird, the gut of a bat is to be used; to join mammal to fish, the gut of an otter; and so forth. The blade employed in the surgery is to be of steel forged in the day and hour of Jupiter and quenched in a mixture of serpent's blood and nettle juice; the knife's handle must be oak, cut during the waning moon from a tree choked with mistletoe. The vital essence of the creatures may be preserved, even when heads must be separated from bodies, by inducing a stupor with an inhalation of steam from a bowl of water infused with henbane.

By use of these techniques, and by uttering incantations which I devised to the purpose, I have created some creatures of most remarkable appearance and capability: a rat with the wings of a hawk, which proved a most voracious predator; a bat with the head of a snake; and many more. I have further been able to recreate creatures of folklore which, if ever they truly existed before, had long since vanished from the Earth: the cockatrice, the gryphon, the hippocampus. It did not prove possible to create hybrids which would breed true to their kind, to my disappointment. The technique might have revealed itself to me in time, but my researches in other, more important directions demanded that I put aside this work.

CHAPTER TWO

THE
HISTORY
OF
MAGIC

Visionary spell and Cave Painting

A considerable number of the earlier entries in the Ruckhurst Manuscript deal with Geoffrey Carlyle's 'history of magic', which he pieced together over several years, from visions evoked with the aid of the demon Astaroth. As happens elsewhere in the manuscript, much of this record is written in the undecipherable code that is believed to be an ancient language, acquired by Rofomagus through occult means. Whilst in his later writings he appears to use this totally cryptic code to disguise certain techniques of Major Summoning, in the history (as far as can be ascertained) he is protecting aspects of the knowledge that he acquired during his consultations with the Magi of the ancient world. Rofomagus, using his control of the demon Astaroth, was able to glimpse, and communicate with, a number of older magical traditions. The earliest of these would seem to be a shaman (Ushun G'shik by name) living during the Paleolithic era (perhaps 30,000 years before Christ) and inhabiting, with his tribe, the limestone caves of what is now Cordoba in Spain.

To view the past is a skill much sought by those who would concern themselves with the lost wisdoms. During my tutelage in Paris, under the powerful guidance of Agrippa, I learned the simple conjuration of image and voice; in a sheet of polished iron, or in the brilliant blade of a knife, by invoking certain powers of air, some simple scrying can be achieved.

These partial visions (no more than the voice of the dead, often the dying cries of a tormented soul) are insufficient to the needs of the necromancer and I sought, and have found, the lines of power, the communion with the living minds of yesteryear.

For the conjuration of the demon Astaroth a time of preparation is needed: of fasting, save for the ingestion of foul water from a stagnant well; of abstinence from all contact with other men; and the body to be daubed with the venom of the common viper, each part of the skin covered. Thus naked, warmed only by a simple brazier fed with the dried roots of henbane, with fresh vervain and oak leaves, and with the dried dung of worms and snakes, two days and nights of silent meditation are required.

For the third day and night the mouth is filled with the litter of the forest, gathered on any third night of a waning moon, and the decay reaches through to the bowels. In this way teeth, tongue and mouth are coated with the odour of waste, the breath of evil. No cleansing should be attempted, for Astaroth disapproves. By this method the Prince's breath, which is the foullest of all demons', will be tolerable to the magus.

Evocation of Astaroth is made from a boat, on a shallow pond or still lake. The surface should be clear, for it is here that the vision will arise; the moon, if there is moon to be seen, should be in its first phase.

The words are, 'A THOREBALO, AROGOGORUABRAO, RETRAGSAMMATHON,

40

Astaroth, who was goddess, who is Demon God, who breathes the waste and litter of the Organism, who is detritus of the Universe, husk and shell of evil, thou greatest of the kelipoth, drawn from the left branch of the life tree, rise up from thy vipers nest, angelic faced one, breathe thy stench of hell upon thy servant Rofomagus, in the name of EMMANUEL, SABAOTH, ADONAI.'

Thus bidden, Astaroth will rise from the lake and will conjure the required vision of the past.

This was my first vision: that of Ushun G'shik, magus of the tribe of the Shiringathok, which dwells in caves and shelters below the high plateau known as Ghostland. A cold place, winds from the north bringing the breath of ice. Legends of the warm lands to the south, across the Eyerock Sea. To this mind, that of the shaman, I could reach only with difficulty, Astaroth's power being weakened by time. But I saw an age before runes or script, an age of painting and bone carving, animals drawn upon the walls of caves in dyes and ochres of various hues, and invested with such power! The magic is beyond me, the subtle influencing of seasons, the changing of migration of herds, the baiting of animals from such silent distance. But from Ushun G'shik I learned of the five ways of closing the eyes, the talent to use thoughts to project influence. This is an art long lost, but surely it can be recaptured by consulting with demons?

I reached astonishing communion with the innocent mind of a boy. He watches how the world is painted, and learns. All his eyes are open. In the same way that I have seen in this vision, so the young have always been trained in the secret arts, and this youth spoke to me of nature, of destiny, of the fear of seasons, of the life of the land, of the power of the nightsmen — the way they call their sorcerers — of the weaving, by mind and ritual, of the fortunes of the tribe.

This way to cause a stag to fall to the huntsman's arrow: at the high part of the day, following the night of a New Moon, mix red ochre (or any red pigment of what I recognise as iron) with the black powder of the ore of manganese. Mix in the dried blood of a stag hunted and killed during the previous moon.

Then paint a stag upon the wall of a holy shrine, at a place where the faded image of your hand, outlined with ochre, can still be seen; use the image of a hand with its first and third finger folded down. This is the sign by which the wind will blow man's scent away from the stag. Draw very faintly the representation of a hunter; draw the hunter's spear in the side of the animal. Call upon the spirit of the stag to depart this particular animal, saying 'MANGASHAR' (Spirit Lord of all Horned Animals), 'DAIANASHIRA' (Spirit daughter of wind and rain), 'THUMUG' (Spirit Lord of the colours of earth) 'run like the wind to a newborn deer, allow blood to spill on tomorrow's hunt. URSCUMOK' (He who inhabits the eyes of man and beast) 'leave the spirit of the stag as I break this bone.'

Snap the sawn-through thigh bone of a young deer, as the eyes are closed in the third way, the words of power reaching to the distant herd.

Oracles

It is quite clear that Rofomagus placed immense importance upon these past visions, plainly seeking in them for 'clues' and 'elements' for some greater magic of his own devising. The technique for summoning Astaroth is demanding and very gruelling, and needed to be repeated for each invocation of the demon. Rofomagus' dedication to the task is evidence enough of its importance to him. Clearly, from the occult wisdom (lost by his own time) gained from cultures as far apart as the Stone Age and the druidic priesthood of later Europe, Rofomagus was able to piece together his own occult philosophy, a spell book of terrifying power and a key to the unlocking not just of demons, but of the more sinister, and more ancient forces of the Universe itself.

He places special importance on the various occult traditions of Bronze Age Greece:

A troublesome vision to evoke, Astaroth greatly reluctant to aid me, yet a vision that filled me with wonder: thus my communication with Plato, whose words live in all men still. From that land of Greece, from the occult thinking of that age, has come a Wisdom as powerful in its content as it is imperfectly preserved in form. I had hoped to increase my knowledge of that Wisdom and I was not disappointed.

We spoke [through the water] of the authority of *reason*, the pureness of abstract knowledge, that which has no need of experiment or material proof. We spoke of the divine character that exists in the simplest idea, in the creation of a single thought. I came to realise that, since ideas dominate the body, the physical world may be manipulated by the very omnipotence of such ideas.

We spoke of the way *all things* in the Universe are *related*, the divine is related to the intellectual, and both relate to the baser earth; I learned much of the way in which the Universe is complete, and is alive, and also of how *each man mimics* the greater Universe: his head is linked to heaven, and the mind of man, in its higher realms, partakes of Divine Wisdom. But this Wisdom is blocked by the lustful, blind passions of the lower mind, the baser part of man. The magus alone can transcend those passions, learning to allow the flow, through his body, of divine knowledge. And the body of man is linked to earth, and from earth flow the baser elements of the organism, the essences of rock and plant.

I found a greater understanding of the divisibility of the Soul. That part of the Soul that is linked to heaven is indivisible, divine; that part of the Soul which is linked to earth is divisible, spreading to reach for earthly power. In this way Man intermingles with the Universal Soul. The World Soul pervades everything and circulates through Man in a way made perfect only by correct understanding of the rhythmic and harmonic motion of the heavenly bodies.

[after a sequence in code] I have striven all my years as an alchemist to glean those essences or *souls* of inanimate objects, for only by controlling the essence of things both base and *superior* can a mortal Man seek to control the higher forces of the Universe. My vision of Plato helped me to comprehend the import of the 'reason'. In a later vision of the magus Agathodorus, I was helped to understand the physical importance of the *maze*.

[sequence in code] venerable sorcerer in the City of Eleusis, presiding over the rites, the worship, of the goddess Demeter, whom I know as Hecate or [obscure]. The rites I saw were complex, much deprivation of the senses, then acute indulgence with imbibings of essential fluids, lambs blood, urine, essence of night flowers. With the eyes closed in what I recognise as the second way, the mind lifted towards the celestial plane, a journey through physical space was taken, an [obscure] a walk of many miles through total darkness, a circular walk, weaving through an area as small as my own workshop. [sequence in code] the traveller was far from home at any point, yet close enough to touch it, and the body became balanced between the farthest and closest point, its rhythm and harmonies an echo of the greater sphere. I observed great power to those who finished the rites; great control.

In a vision of the oracle at Delphi I noticed the correct form of ritual for the closing of the eyes in the fourth way, that which allows a glimpse of future time (although scrying the future is a hard task for me even now). I learned much of the ways of divination during my fifty evocations of Astaroth. I glimpsed the familiar spirits, so potent now as helpers in animal form, but once just formless demons, able to cry out the future on a simple command. I saw the pickled head of Orpheus, in its temple on the solitary Isle of Lesbos, and heard its terrible keening cry, the dead voice still magically prophetic. In the burning entrails of domestic animals I could see some simple indications, but these and the languages of birds, and of snakes, even the whispering of trees, all these were techniques that held little relevance to my own quest, and I gave them scant attention. Men about to die, if asked questions of the future, seemed to glimpse that future as their life blood spilled; this will be investigated more. But at Delphi I witnessed a true alchemy between man, fire and earth, causing a powerful foretelling of future events, and I learned certain controls that will aid my final quest.

In Rofomagus' manuscript there appear copious sketches of the oracle at Delphi, from which this reconstruction has been made. The image must have been a powerful one for the magus, for he describes it in great detail:

I was able to smell the sharp odour of the olive groves that cluster on these lower slopes of Mount Parnassus, steep, boulder-strewn slopes, enclosing numerous clefts and grottos in the hill. The oracle is in the form of a pit, that opens in the face of the grey rock and emits a sulphurous, yet clarifying vapour. A small Apollonic temple stands nearby, and here I have witnessed the cruellest of sacrifices to the wise God. The oracle speaks through a woman, whose majesty and sagacity are scarce matched by her physical perfection. She is called 'Pythia', and awaits the questions seated on a gold, three-legged stool. In consultation with the oracle she writhes as if in a fit, her neck swollen, entranced and blind to those who wait.

Celtic Magic and Merlin

Much of Rofomagus' documented visionary history of magic is concerned with the Celtic ritual magic, earth magic and shamanism that would have formed a basis for his own medieval ritual. His greatest interest was in the transformation, or *shape-shifting*, of man into his animal nature, an act that took the essence of man both into a baser form, the instinctive animal, and into a higher form, for the animals of nature were the embodiments of the gods.

I have witnessed shamanistic transformation into bull, stag, hare, boar, cat, heron, crane, even into fish. In the form of a swan, a prince may pursue a princess, and this is a common form of magic courtship. Wrongdoers are locked into animal shape and left to wander the forests alone, at the mercy of hunters. Witches commonly haunt village and fort in the form of crow, or raven.

The phenomenon was a psycho-physical change, which followed a ritual fasting, a great deal of 'suggestion', and the tainting of blood through the infusion of herbal extracts. Rofomagus was clearly witnessing an advanced form of what we might call a 'collective dream state', wherein past and present, and psychic and physical realities merged to form a bridge between the divine and the animal aspects of man.

One of the most fascinating descriptions in this part of the manuscript, however, concerns the druidic summoning of the Horned God of the Celts, the Lord of Animals. In his manuscript, Rofomagus writes the name as *Erananog*. We know of *Cernunnos*, later familiar as (H)Erne the Hunter:

The Horned Man of the tribes is both hunter and hunted. In this I can see the way man, animal and God are linked, for as man hunts so he is the spirit of the hunted, and the spirit of his deity. I am reminded of the horned shaman of the primitive Shiringathok tribe. I witnessed the invocation of Erananog by the people of Belinanix, of the tribe of the Eburones. The magi of this people do not use a room of stone, or some hidden chamber for their magic, but rather a glade in the woods, which they call a *nemeton*, between ancient stands of oak and ash. They plant hawthorn if this tree is absent from the site. In trees such as these, and rowan, elder, hazel and willow, they conceive of the spirits of the dead as living on, and these elemental forces have given me much study, for they exist in my own time, but have changed their nature. In the enigmatic stones that rise, such as at Stonehang and Avebury they see spirits also, but these I am unable to contact, perhaps because of the exorcism of the previous centuries that was practised upon them. The earth of these people of the Eburones teems with life, and without recourse to complicated spells and symbol markings they can pass into that life, and out again.

The elders of these ancient necromancers are called *druid*, and they are the custodians of vision and prophecy, sacrifice, poetic lore, the ritual calendar of seasons, and the law itself. They are all-powerful, revered by the Chieftains, and sleep with the daughters of Kings to induce clear prophecy. Their training in the magic and prophetic art lasts half a lifetime, for nothing is ever written; all of history, all of magic, all of law being held in the mind, and spoken only between magus and student. They learn first the poetic history, then the basic law of the tribe, then the medical sciences. But that sacred, secret mystery is long denied them, the knowledge that will give them power over nature. The simplicity of that sacred knowledge, relating to the Breath and the Word, is deceptive, for without recourse to the conjuration of demons the Celtic magus can visit the afterlife, and the territory of the Gods.

In my vision of the people of Belinanix and their magical practice I witnessed human sacrifice of a most appalling nature, the victim selected by lottery, yet succumbing to the iron blade or the strangling rope with a sense of honour and delight that in my own practice can only be induced with stupefying liquors. Their veneration of the human head is fully as intense as I have learned from books. The head is the source of divinity, of courage, and of power, and these qualities are not lost in death. The skulls of the honoured dead of the tribe are the eyes, ears and mouths through which the gods of the four seasons watch, listen, and speak of future things. The heads of courageous enemies are sources of power for he who possesses the grim trophy, and these are placed at the hearth of houses, or below the eaves, to ward off spirits, and make battle cry to drive away hags and the ghosts of the restless dead. Much cherished, the heads of Kings and Princes are kept in cedar oil in wooden chests, and before battle a warrior will sleep with the head below his sword hand.

The shamans fashion wooden idols, marking each statue with the blood, hair or brain — and thus the presence — of a dead warrior; in this way the warrior gods are brought close.

They do not celebrate a year of seasons, but rather celebrate three years.

The nine months between each season's feast is related to the magic growth of life in the fertile bellies of the women. Autumn's harvest is followed by a summer's fertility, and spring's thanksgiving by winter's new beginning.

But in the oak glades, close to the stones of the fairy folk, the druid practice a natural magic of potent and awesome effect. They use herbs and extracts of earth which are well familiar to me, and utilise the anger of the sprites and forest spirits to ferment a magic brew which will attract the gods. Of great importance in all their potions is mistletoe, cut from an oak branch on the sixth night of the waxing moon, and trimmed with a knife fashioned from gold, which is incorruptible and will not cause release of the moon that is trapped in the berries. Witnessed by warriors who have survived wounds mortal to most, and crying out the ancient words in spells that are charged with terrifying power, so come the gods and demons to the control of the shamans.

Thus is summoned Erananog, the Lord of Animals, by the burning of an iron blade on a fire of hawthorn and ashwood, censed with catkin from a young hornbeam, sap of a dogwood stem, the fur of a buck deer, berries and herbs from the glade, and the juice of mistletoe; by the sacrificing of a new-born goat, which is astonishingly returned to life by the beneficent deity; and by the crying of the following words:

> Stone glade in oak wood, ash branch into warrior head,
> Smoke of hawthorn chokes the hags of air,
> Hear the flight of winter geese, the running of the wounded boar,
> Hear the clash of brave iron in the name of the Lord of Animals,
> Hear the breathing of the god, rampant and fertile,
> Hear the footfall of the antlered god,
> Hear Erananog enter the stone glade in oak wood...

This invocation is repeated, the fire struck with a staff of ash marked with the name Erananog, until at length the shape of the Lord of Animals will appear at the periphery of the glade, and may be asked for favour.

In this fashion may words and prophesies be called from the head of an enemy, preserved in oil:

Anoint the open eyes of the head with celandine, field daisy and ground ivy, clarified and mixed with the sap of mistletoe leaf and powdered oak bark. Touch the juice of rowan berry mixed with eel bile and ram's urine to the ears of the head. Open the mouth of the head and place mandrake upon the tongue so that a voice may be heard. Hold the head so that the eyes see to the North. Let the scent of blood from a man killed in recent battle touch the nose of the head and bring it to angry presence. Say 'AMARA EOCH, ATREBATHETOCH, MOGOCHFILABIX, TEUTATHERION, Great Warrior, whose arm never tired, whose legs ran only towards battle, whose iron was feared by whole armies, whose head is more powerful than a hundred warriors, find voice to speak of N.'

Towards the end of his History, Rofomagus writes of the strangest vision that he was able to evoke with the aid of the demon Astaroth, that of the legendary Merlin, the late Romano-British magician whose druidic practices represented the final form of Celtic magic.

The tradition of the legend is strong, that of Arthur and his Knights portrayed in colourful story and fairy tale. Yet an older tradition, preserved in the writings of the magi, and in the secret tongue, records a necromancer of great power, who was also a bard and lived for many generations. His name was Merlin, and became Myrddin, and he lived for two centuries and more, defying death with a spell of awesome power. His final killing, in the dark lands north of the great Wall, was at the hands of the demon which I would call Marchosias.

My vision of Merlin was not easy to evoke, and I learned much of the way Time and Man will induce change in the reality of past. To such an extent has the life of this great magus been shaped by legend, that his true life has slipped almost out of the grasp of time and the demon Astaroth. There is a shadow world that exists beside our own, and the true Merlin lives in memory therein; the creature of myth that exists in the past of our own world is a mere *fetch*, without mind, without existence. It was necessary to penetrate that veil of shadow to touch the mind of lost Merlin.

To do so I had first to obtain an iron sword that had been used at the time of Merlin, and on which traces of blood yet remained. Such a sword I found by excavating in a death mound near to Barrowhill and Avebury. Using a fragment of the grey stone that stands at Avebury, the name of Merlin/Myrddin was inscribed upon this corroded blade, my own blood mixed with the brown dust. The blade was held across the lake water, while I called in the secret way of the people of Iron, saying, 'TEUTATHERION, TARANITHECTON, EPONISTA, BRIGGATHERION, ELUGADENITHAM, however ye may be, whether demon, god or elemental, I thee charge to tie my vision to Merlin, by the power of OAK, ASH and THORN, and the blade of IRON, BRONZE and STONE'. Then, by invoking the hidden skull of the dead magus, and the intervention of the spirit of the great Arthur, whom I addressed as Artorian, Dragonlord of the Britons, I achieved the breaching of the shadow wall.

The vision that formed was brief and rewarding. I regarded Merlin, an old man, nearly a hundred years of age, crouched in the torch-lit chamber near to the sea wherein he performed his magic art. This place, which was empty to the eyes of mortal men who might wander from the shore into its gloomy confines, was bedecked with shields and swords, lances, cups and helmets, the great armour and treasure of a thousand years of the Britons. Great wolfhounds slept peacefully in the warmth of burning oak logs. Merlin, aware of my presence, said very little, but allowed me to observe as he cured the death wound of the warlord Arthur, a wound attained in skirmishing against Irish reivers on the coast of Cornwall. It was not, at this time, the moment for Arthur's death. I saw the body of Arthur and knew that his grave, at ravaged Glastonbury, was his true resting place, for the man was unnaturally tall, and of the build of a bear.

His sword was long, curve-bladed in the way of his ancestors, yet he was marked in the fashion of the Roman: in the manner of his leather girdle and tunic, the leather cuirass, the thick, skin greaves, decorated with iron studs. A noble man, the wound in his heart was closed by the ministrations of the magus. The death that was thwarted was then taken upon Merlin himself, and the necromancer aged before my eyes, his body weakening, his skin turning to the colour of a corpse, the bones in his body standing out proud. And yet, still Merlin was filled with a magic vigour. This manner of absorbing the death of another I studied with care. The embrocation was the powdered root of black mandrake mixed with wolf bane, vipers bugloss, the tips of burdock, orpine, the long lived herb, and vervain to ward off the eyes of evil. This was worked to a salve and then bound with sulphur, the blood of the common spider and the white paste from the gut of a seabird. I knew this to be effective in closing wounds, but by the addition of lichen scraped from the dawn face of a stone erected above the corpse of a warrior, the wound closed all the way to the heart.

By mingling their blood, through the wrist of the left arm, the possessing spirit of death passed from Arthur to Merlin. To reduce the power of death in his own body, Merlin then allowed his arm to be savaged by the smaller of the hounds, which he provoked to fury by beating it with a bronze rod. The beast, snapping at the wizard's arm, was instantly possessed, then slaughtered by the magus and burned on the oak fire. The spirit danced in torment within the smoke, but could do no more than return to hell. Yet Merlin retained part of the poison of death, building in his body each time he performed this most astonishing of resurrections. In this way his pact with the demon Marchosias, whom he called Menapothan Ra, was weakened, and he came that much closer to being possessed most terribly. But I learned of the secret names of Marchosias, and the true pattern of the seal that will keep this demon at bay, and this was a remarkable knowledge, remarkably learned.

There is a post-script in code:

As the hour of Mars was reached so the vision faded. And Merlin turned to me and spoke most powerfully, and in a strange tongue, saying, 'Thy place is known to me. Thou art a sorcerer upon the mound of He who once walked the Earth, the three-horned One who is fallen, Lufugus. Thy place is of great mystery and of terrible power, and it is haunted and not even I would dare to walk upon it. Thou should know that those who built the temple had the power to summon the greatest of the Fallen. Thou art doomed by their spirits.'

CHAPTER THREE

MAGICAL CREATURES AND DEMONS

Earth Sprites and Minor Demons

As above, so below: the simple philosophy of the alchemist pervades Rofomagus' manuscript. By controlling and influencing the elements and elementals of base earth, so a certain control and influence could be exerted upon the divine forces of the higher sphere. The alchemist studied the inanimate, seeking to release the elemental power from minerals and earth; the cabalist sought to understand and control the elementals of animate nature, the sprites, demons and 'fairies' that inhabited earth and wood, air, fire and water.

Of the realm of earth and air there are many thousands of sprites and spirits; of water there are fewer, and fire fewer still (but these are malevolent and hard to

influence). Their names are manifold, but these are the names given them by man, which is less secret than their real names (which to know means to control). These are the sprites with which I have dealt most successfully: boggles, bloody-bones, shellycoats, hags, nightbats, scrags, fantasms, hobgoblins, hobhoulards, dobbies, kelpies, satyrs, pans, fauns, spoorns, men-in-the-oak, fire-drakes, melch-dicks, picksgillies, hobby-lanthorns, knockers, mad-tuttles, old-shocks, tutgots, sprets, spunks, tantarrabobs, scar-bugs, shag-foals, bolls, wraithes, waffs, gallytrots, imps, gringes, bonelesses, hudskins, hell-wains, mawkins, kobbolds, lubberkins, thrummy caps, cutties and banshees.

These creatures are often invisible, and vary in malignancy from those that will maliciously trick and destroy a traveller, to those more inclined to aid him. Terrestrial devils, or sprites of earth, are those genii, Dryads, Faunes, Lares, Satyrs, Woodnymphs, Foliots, Fairies and Robin Goodfellows which are both conversant with men, and yet do harm to them unless they are controlled. In times of old the Heathen Peoples were in great awe of these demons, and revered them as Astarte, Baal, Isis and Osiris, Dagon and the rest.

On heathers and greens these sprites dance at night, leaving the green circles whereon it is dangerous for a man to tread. A bigger kind of sprite, much inhabiting woodlands, are the Hobgoblins and Robin Goodfellows, and these may be induced to grind corn, milk goats, cut wood, or do any manner of drudgery work. They will mend old and rusted iron, losing their fear of such metal in exchange for becoming a familiar spirit and treated well.

Some of these sprites are forlorn and lost, inhabiting deserted houses and broken woods with ruins. These are commonly called Foliots and they may be commanded by a simple spell and are of use to the magician. They will make strange noises in the night, howl pitifully and then laugh again, cause flames and sudden light, fling stones, rattle chains, open and shut doors; they appear in the likeness of hares, crows and black dogs.

Of very great value to the magus are those subterranean sprites that inhabit caves, passages and mines. Although invisible to man, by their knocking they can indicate the presence of a lode, or of buried treasure. When seen they are ugly, like short, malformed children, dressed in ragged clothes stolen from the bodies of dead miners. They are not dangerous, but to gain their co-operation apples and cheese must be left as a repast, iron must be left for them to make new tools, five small birds in a cage must be given, and your own name marked on a piece of ore, or subterranean stone, along with the cry repeated twenty times into the gloom of, 'This is I, N., who gives these gifts; lead me to fortune or safety.'

Of those minor demons not bound to any element I have exercised control over one hundred and fourteen, by learning of their names, and devising seals to control them. These are the names and general use of those which may be summoned to assist with necromancy and the pursuit of vigour and longevity.

Marogath, who will sting like an insect and can induce stupor, is controlled by the dust of a butterfly wing and fungal spores and used to locate the secretly buried dead. Golgathasta, quite malicious and poisonous to touch, like some amphibious creatures, can be controlled by striking with a pouch of lizard skin containing powdered skull of frogs or newts; used for discouraging Merrows and other malevolent water sprites during the resurrection of a drowned man. Rocogrimus, who is most dangerous and will disguise himself as a calm horse, can ride below the earth and bring out hidden roots, ores and elements for the greater concoction of spells and is controlled with a cross made of rowan, tied with the hair of a water horse. Sleem, a night flier, can assist with night passage undertaken by magic means. Obeys in exchange for a blood feast on a child. Mogana is of female form, but with her hands reversed. She is not a succubus, but may be induced to seduce the unwary and gather nails, hair, tears or other body matter for use in cursing and the like. She is controlled by powdered mandrake and garlic, and can only be summoned by the voice of a child invoking the maid-servants of Diana.

A smaller type of sprite, often malicious, are those connected with the tiny plants and herbs with which a cabalist dealt for magical purposes:

The herbs of Thyme and Sage have potent, angry sprites, sage useful for promoting long life and increasing understanding and thyme being a balm for coughing complaints, melancholia, and essential in spells to induce these complaints. Replace the herbs with beeswax and calf blood.

Comfrey will effect cure in broken bones, wounds and sores, and its sprite is benign, satisfied with powdered bone sprinkled into the root hole.

Those sprites of fungus, especially bark fungus, can grow like a mole upon the body for revenge. Replace plucked fungus with the decayed corpse of a small bird, bark fungus with a sliver of hawthorn.

The sprites of Henbane, Hecate, Hemlock and Hellbore are demons which can cause wild dreams, fits, strokes, or induce stupor and quiescence, and they must be subdued with iron, blood and magic. Henbane is essential in all spells to induce convulsions. Hemlock is a deadly poison, but smeared on the hands allows *far touch*.

The sprite of Aconite can shoot poisoned darts, the juice of this plant being a potent poison. As with Belladonna, which can reduce pain and swelling or induce them in magic ways, upon plucking the sprites must be subdued with some small, dead creature.

The sprites of Daisy, Primrose, and Bluebell, all required for love philtres, or inducing friendship, are gentle, but are protected by the Dryads of Oak, which will cause harm upon you unless they are subdued; replace the plants with corn biscuit, or milk droplets, or fatty cheese.

Replace Motherwort with crushed rowan berry baked into the centre of a dough made from wild grasses and hazel nut. Motherwort is used to induce weakness in women or the heart, or can be used to cure these things.

Vervain has an amorous sprite, who is also malevolent and under the control of witches. Of use in love potions, this herb must be taken only in the hour of Venus, and replaced with semen.

The list in the grimoire is seemingly endless, but Rofomagus has a strong warning about that most potent and dangerous of plants: Mandragora, or Mandrake:

I have learned that mandrake is named from the language of the first men, *mandragora* meaning 'that which is of the red star' which I take to be Mars. Because of its similarity to the body it is possessed of a powerful demon, and exists half in Hell and half in the Earth. The mandrake which is male is white, with scented blossom and yellow berries, and leaves that spread on the ground. The sprite will induce stupor, delirium, insanity and death if the plant is pulled and eaten without proper precaution. The female mandrake is black, her root widely forked. Both kinds of mandrake will scream if pulled from the ground.

To remove a mandrake, first cut the ground with an iron sword, or knife, three circles around the plant. Whisper erotica to the plant at all times. Face always to the west, and do this in the hour of Mars, but on the day of Venus. Attach the plant by string to the neck of a black dog, and then attract the dog with meat so that it runs and pulls the mandrake from the ground. The dog will be killed by its screech. Block your ears with wax against this cry. Fill the hole with a clay mannikin, in which you have placed the semen of a hanged man and the seal of the demon Asmodeus scratched on a piece of animal skin. Drench the mannikin with the dog's blood before placing it in the earth with the words: 'SINAH, ITADA, NAMAN, ADANI, HANIS, thy power to my life, thy hatred to this figure.'

Woodland Magic and Valkyries

Woods, woodland and the open spaces in them have always been of central importance to the magician; all trees have some sacred or demonic association, beliefs living on from early times. Indeed, Geoffrey Carlyle seems to have spent a considerable part of his early years in documenting the woodland in the vicinity of his house, and in subduing the natural forces that resided within them. Oak, ash and thorn (hawthorn and blackthorn) are probably the most potent tree types, and oak especially has an ancient history of use in secret arts. Even Rofomagus' journal on the subject of tree sprites begins with the folk rhyme, 'Demonne folk are in Old Oaks'. Oak coppices are the haunt of a particularly vindictive and snaring sprite known as the Man-in-the Oak, or Oakman. Rofomagus subdued these spirits:

A pierced stone, daubed with the berry of mistletoe and hung on a soaked twig of oak; this carried round the neck, and the words 'DRYON, RYOT, DRUN, PANATASTACOR-AN', will subdue the Men-in-the-Oak.

Rofomagus' manuscript is full of short rhymes, leftovers from an older wisdom: Elm do grieve, Oak do hate, Willow do walk, if you travels late.

Elm should be cut but rarely, for other elms pine and grieve; but its bark, especially from the root, is useful for inducing melancholy and wasting sadness. Oaks bitterly resent being cut and coppiced, and a coppice springing from a felled oak wood will be malevolent and dangerous. The most stringent safeguards are necessary if one is to pass through it, especially if it is a bluebell wood, which can suck the traveller into the ground. Willows will uproot themselves and pursue a traveller, muttering. Willow sap, and leaves crushed with sloeberry, will cause a man to be haunted and ever aware of being pursued.

When Oak, Ash and Hawthorn grow close together, especially in threes, a twig taken from each, bound with a red thread from your garment, is the most effective protection against night spirits when walking through woodland. Also powerful protection against such fairies and demons is the wood of Ash, fashioned into a staff or cross. Ash will protect stables from blight, and crops from malicious influence. Rowan is also powerful against demons and witches, and evil forces sent against the wearer: twigs of Rowan tied and carried round the neck, or a branch carved into a gnarled staff will drive all evil forces away; the juice of the red berries can heal wounds inflicted by malicious sprites.

Hawthorn is lucky, especially if growing solitary, and the sprite associated with it is benevolent, but not if brought inside the house. Hawthorns growing in a ring of three have powerful magical properties, but the sprites must be controlled more fiercely.

Hazel is a tree which is a source of wisdom and of fertility; the nuts may be used in divination, especially to know of ones future family; a staff of Hazel can hurt and punish troublesome demons. Apple trees, if carefully grown, will effect power and youthfulness, but the sprites associated with Apple are female, winsome, and will carry away a sleeping man who has not guarded himself carefully with a Rowan cross.

Satyrs are among the most capricious and unpredictable of the forest entities, in appearance half goat and half man, with cloven hooves, pointed ears and hairy bodies, yet with the features of those primitive animals found in the Far East that so resemble man: the monkeys. They are often to be heard chasing nymphs through the woods, although their presence can more often be noted by the bird-like music that they pipe. They are less familiar in this country because of their dislike of rain. Of more sinister aspect are the Dryads, which haunt oak glades and often disguise themselves in the trunks of the trees themselves. They are female, and of great beauty, wearing oakleaves in their hair, and thin robes. But they carry axes and will mortally punish any traveller who harms their trees. They can often be seen dancing through the forest, and may be kept at bay by the simple expedient of holding an acorn in a container of fresh earth. If their respect is won (say by preventing a tree being cut by a forester) they will lead the magus to that mistletoe which is most potently influenced by the planets.

The elementals of air are confusing and elusive, and are made manifest as birds and clouds, although they may shift their shape into the fashion of winged females, of varying beauty from those of enticing, rapturous brilliance, to the most evil of air hags. In different times these elementals have been known by different names, and shaped by the belief and reveration of those on earth below — as *Harpies* they seemed as hags, with long, pointed ears, and the bodies of carrion birds, which would swoop upon mortals and torment them. The *Chimaera* has the head of a lion and the body of a goat, and it resides in storm clouds and stirs them into turmoil. As *Valkyries* these spirits are graceful, and found haunting pools and lakes in lonely forests where they appear as swans. But they shift shape and can be found riding the wind above a battle, selecting those warriors who shall die, and carrying their spirits to the Otherworld. To obtain part of the plumage of such an elemental is to force her to do your will, but to try and steal such a feather is to court death, for Valkyries are warrior elementals of great accomplishment. Also presiding over battle, taunting and holding back the swords of the enemy and carrying off the souls of the dead, are the Screech Hags, the *Macha*, the *Morrigan* and the *Badb*, three warrior elementals, once worshipped as goddesses. They can be summoned easily after any battle, or skirmish, and appear as ravens, screech owls, jackdaws or any carrion crow.

Fire and Water Elementals

The elementals of fire are most enigmatic and mysterious, and are truly beyond proper human comprehension. They dwell in the upper realms of the atmosphere, and never descend to Earth. They are like shapes glimpsed in a flickering fire, having no consistent form. Theirs is a cold fire, but it may burn hotly if they desire, consuming any creature rash enough to ascend into their domain. Few are bold enough to risk their wrath. No bird can fly so high, but a witch or magus being transported by occult means may move high above the clouds, and if unprepared may be burned to death and fall from the sky in a trail of flame. The fire elementals may be tamed by the use of certain Pentacles, but even this is a hazardous undertaking, and the wise magician will simply avoid their realm.

Equally mysterious are those creatures of the upper air termed *lucifugum*, which to say, fly-the-light. Malignant and restless, they roam the sky at night and will pursue and kill those incautious enough to travel after dark. They may be controlled more readily, but this rouses them to greater hatred, and extreme care must be used lest they evade control and take a terrible revenge.

Water Devils are those Naiades or Nymphs which inhabit water, both sea and lake, and cause Chaos. These cause Inundations, many times Shipwrecks, and deceive men in divers ways, as Succubi, or otherwise, appearing for the most part in women's shapes. It is said that they will consort with mortal men, but that upon some dislike or disagreement, will return to the water, and trick the man to come with them, and drown. Those of legend who have so consorted are Aegeria, Diana, Ceres and the like. Two Scottish Lords of fame, Mackbeth and Banco, did sacrifice to the wise women who had told them their fortunes, and who had used hydromantaeia, or divination by waters.

Among the most evil of water elementals is the corpse of a drowned man that is inhabited by a demon; until the body is decayed, this fearsome apparition will swim after ships, or walk upon the land, and act as an agent of destruction to all whom it encounters. A simple exorcism may rid the corpse of the possessing spirit. These must be distinguished from Blue Men, who inhabit the underwater caves off the rugged north coast of these isles. These too will swim after ships and pull them down, but they may be effectively driven off by a rhyming insult; he who gains the last line, whether elemental or Captain, shall win the encounter.

Also in the wild north may be found the Marool, the most malevolent of the sea-demons, who takes the form of a fish, and has a crest of flickering flame and eyes all over his head. He often appears in the wild sea foam when it is phosphorescent. He delights in storms, and helps make them worse, and cries wildly and exultantly when some poor ship goes under. The Marool is beyond control.

I have had much discourse with Selkies, which may be found in all calmer waters. These are ancient folk of the land who have been banished to the sea by witchcraft. They disguise themselves as seals, wearing seal-skins, and in this way are able to breathe below the water. They are beautiful, and non-malevolent, and sometimes come ashore to co-habit with terrestrial humans; the offspring of such concourse are webbed of feet and hands, dim-witted and ugly. They can help in the understanding of the Asrai, or water fairies, a most useful elemental, but one whose language is incomprehensible. They are commonly dredged up by fishermen and plead to be set free, and will melt to nothing within a few hours. Beautiful to regard, their skin is ice cold, and their touch will burn for life, but they are rarely malevolent.

The same is not true of Mermaids, which manifest as human above the waist, and fish below; of great beauty in their human guise, their appearance in the sea about a ship presages a storm or a wreck. Also known as Merrows, the females are of surpassing beauty, with flowing, golden hair, white gleaming arms, and dark, enticing eyes. Male Merrows are hideous, with green hair and green teeth, and eyes akin to the tiny eyes of pigs; their noses are long and red, and their arms short and flipper-like. All mere-folk wear red caps of seal skin to enable them to live in the water.

All these sprites of water may be summoned in the following manner: strike at the water with nine lengths of green weed, tied into a rope; when the foam appears that presages the arrival of the elemental, offer it crumbs of a cake baked with dried sea-salt, crushed shell of sea-snail and crab, and the dried, powdered bone of a drowned man. When the elemental comes to you protect yourself with a cross made from sea-wrack, nailed through with iron and tied around with bristles from the carcase of a whale.

If taken by the Marool, guard against possession by a sea-corpse by invoking NAMA, ASTU, ASTAROTH, CERES and LEVIATHAN in the drowning breath.

To travel to far lands by sea is to risk the elemental Sirens, of which there are many, their voices sweet and seductive, and capable of enchanting the traveller and luring him to the rocks. With the head and shoulders of beautiful women, their bodies are those of birds whose wings have been clipped; they haunt the shores of rocky isles and may be subdued by music of equal beauty, or by causing the sound of a storm to fill the air.

Of fresh water nymphs there are abundant numbers, of brooks, springs and stagnant waters. These are on the whole benevolent elementals, and assist in curing the sick, watching over flowers, fields, and flocks. Many have the gift of prophecy and those that live not in the deep water but in grottoes nearby can deliver oracles. They are young in appearance, and beautiful, feeding on the nectar of flowers, and the sweet substances of nature.

Major Demons

The main work of a magus lay in the summoning and control of the major Princes of the Descending Hierarchy — that is to say, the important demons of Hell. This was evidently the most important task Rofomagus set himself, to achieve a more complete control than any magus before him. He describes at length the many such creatures he had succeeded in subduing to his will.

I have directed my efforts these many years towards mastery of all three-score and ten demons whose characteristics are set forth in the *Lemegeton*. Through the control of one of these great Princes any desired consequence may be produced, but in truth there is little purpose in evoking a major presence to achieve an effect workable through some simpler magic, for the preparations are stringent and lengthy and the operation is invariably exhausting.

I have described the manner in which the magus must prepare himself and make ready the instruments of the art. When he is ready to begin the ceremony he must thoroughly fumigate the summoning chamber by burning a mixture of laurel juice, camphor, salt, white resin and sulphur.

The circle, which differs for each operation, may be drawn in chalk or, in certain instances where figures of especial power are to be evoked, formed of strips of goatskin secured with iron nails drawn from a child's coffin. The circle must also be traced with the knife of the art. A mixture of substances must be burned in the brazier according to the sign under which the operation is to be performed. Under Jupiter a blend of aloes wood, ash, cedar, ambergris, powdered lapis lazuli, saffron, storax, peacock's feathers, stork's blood and stag's brain is to be used. When the preparations are complete the magus dons his robe, while uttering the formula:

> By the mysterious power of this garment I put on the armour of salvation in the strength of the Most High, ANCOR, AMICAR, AMIDES, THEODONIAS, ANITOR, that my purpose be achieved, O ADONAI, through thy power, to whom be honour and glory for evermore.

The ceremony now proceeds, and when the magus is experienced and forceful in his adjurations the required demon will frequently appear as soon as the initial formula of invocation is uttered. Sometimes he is reluctant to manifest himself — I have often found Asmodeus particularly so, and a further incantation is required, containing dire threats:

> If you do not obey promptly and without tarrying I will shortly increase your torments for one thousand years in Hell. I constrain you therefore to appear here in comely human shape, by the Most High Names of God, HAIN, LON, HILAY, SABAOTH, HELIM, RADISHA, LEDIEHA, ADONAY, JEHOVAH, YAH, TETRAGRAMMATON, SADAI, MESSIAS, AGIOS, ISCHYROS, EMMANUEL, AGLA, Jesus who is ALPHA and OMEGA, the beginning and the end, that you be

justly established in the fire, having no power to reside, habit or abide in this place henceforth: and I require your doom by the virtue of the said names, that St Michael drive you to the uttermost of the infernal abyss.

Should even this fail after being thrice repeated, a third and more terrible conjuration, invoking the seven secret names ADONAI, PERAI, TETRAGRAMMATON, ANEXNEXETON, INESSENSATOAL, PATHUMATON and ITEMON may be used. If even this does not bring the demon forth — as has happened but once in my experience — the Curse of the Chains may be called into force. The demon's name and seal are put into a box along with divers foetid substances. The box is tied with iron wire to bind the demon, and is held over the fire on the point of the sword while the words of the Curse are uttered, concluding with:

As thy name and seal are bound in this box, choked with sulphurous substance and about to burn in this material fire, so in the Name of JEHOVAH and by the power and dignity of the three Names TETRAGRAMMATON, ANEXHEXETON, PRIMEMATUM, may all these drive thee into the lake of fire prepared for the damned and accursed spirits, to remain there until the Day of Wrath, no more

remembered before the face of God who shall come to judge the quick and the dead with the whole world by fire.

As the box is thrust into the flames, so the recalcitrant demon will appear.

At all times the demon, once summoned, must be spoken to pleasantly and with fullest control. He may be obstinate and ill-tempered, or may lie. Truthful answers may be extracted by further adjurations, accompanied by thrusts of the wand into the brazier; but if the magus loses patience with the demon, or becomes angry, he runs the grave risk of being lured into errors which may cost him his soul. Some authorities counsel the use of sacrifice during the operation as a means to control intractable or surly demons, but this may produce a fatal distraction, and is a most inadvisable procedure.

Rofomagus goes on to describe all the demons he has thus summoned. As in the grimoires he assigned them ranks and titles on an apparently arbitrary basis. A few examples will suffice to convey the flavour.

Asmodeus is a most strong and powerful King, though most reluctant to be summoned. He has three heads: the first like that of a bull, the second like a ram, the third that of a man. His body is human but he has a serpent's tail and his feet are webbed, like those of a diving bird. His breath is fiery. He carries in one hand a lance, and in the other a pennon. He is most expert in arithmetic and astronomy, and gives true and full answers to questions on these subjects. He may make a man invisible, or reveal the site of hidden treasures.

Baal is a Prince most evil to behold. His body is that of a spider, with eight legs; he has the heads of a man, a toad and a cat. He is a most expert tutor in matters of lechery and sensuality, and may tempt the weak magus into a fondness for luxury which will destroy his ability as a practitioner of the Art.

Glasyalabolas is a demon most familiar to me. His form is human, like a man of middle years, ordinarily dressed and distinguished in appearance; he might be a scholar at court. But he also has wings, like those of a giant bat, and when he speaks it can be seen that he has the teeth of a hunting dog, which make it hard to comprehend his speech. He teaches the arts and sciences, and is most learned and persuasive. it would be easy to make the error of regarding him as a sympathetic spirit, and in my youth I was perilously close to doing so, before Agrippa reminded me that if I so much as breached the circle with my finger those teeth would eagerly tear me to pieces, and carry the fragments into Hell.

Astaroth appears in the form of an angel, but far from being beautiful has a countenance of unearthly evil. He rides upon a dragon and carries in his hand a viper, but on command will assume plain human guise. His breath is stinking and foul, and poisonous to any who inhale it; therefore the magus must make especial precautions to protect against this eventuality. Astaroth reveals the past, to which purpose I have summoned him many times, and will also explain in great detail how the spirits fell, and most particularly how his own downfall came about.

Belial is a most powerful Duke; he is the Prince of Lies and Deceit. In form he is like a man of great depravity; he rides a chariot of fire. His greatest talent is in the fomenting of wickedness, and in causing guilt to arise in the hearts of men. His joy is in causing anguish. He will not answer truthfully unless some offering is made to him.

Phoenix is a Marquis who appears in the shape of the fiery bird, but on command will adopt human form. His voice is clear and melodious, like that of a child, but the magus must take care not to heed its blandishments. He is knowledgeable in science, and is accomplished as a poet. Although not a demon of great power, he is unusual in his willingness to do the magus's bidding. He hopes that one day, a thousand years from now, he will be restored to his throne; thus he eschews the worst evil of other demons.

Vassago is a Duke of human form, excepting his head, which is like a skull, triangular in shape and the colour of bone. His eyes are slanted and reach nearly to the temples. He is expert at promoting lewdness and vice of all kinds, and will discourse on these at great length.

Agares had the form of an old man. He carries a goshawk on his wrist, and rides astride a great crocodile. He can reveal the future, but he speaks in impenetrable riddles and cannot be relied upon to speak the truth; nor is it possible to determine whether he is lying until long after he has been discharged.

Lucifuge Rofocale is the great Prime Minister of the Descending Hierarchy, and the Master of Pacts. Upon his shaven head sit three long and twisted horns; his eyes are immense, like those of some nocturnal creature; his legs are bandy and hooved, resembling a satyr; and he has a tail. He may readily be summoned, though will always complain at the disturbance of his rest. He will offer a pact whereby he will do the magus's bidding on occasion, in exchange for the promise of his soul in twenty or fifty years' time. It is possible for the clever magus to outwit him, and make a pact whose wording allows him to keep his soul. I have done more: by the use of most powerful adjurations, clues to which I found in my scrying of the past, I have compelled the great Lucifuge Rofocale to set his seal to a pact whereby he must do my bidding at all times, without complaint, and without promise of reward. Thus do I claim the name of Rofomagus.

After the demon has done what is required of it, the magus should bid it depart with these words:

> O spirit N, because thou hast answered my demands I hereby licence thee to depart, without doing injury to man or beast. Go, I say, but be ready and willing to come whenever duly conjured by the sacred rites of magic. I conjure thee to withdraw in peace, and may the peace of God ever continue between me and thee.

The demon will require no second bidding, and as the last words are spoken will vanish, leaving behind only its characteristic stink.

Incubus/Succubus

Many cultures have traditions concerning unearthly and evil spirits which take the form of extraordinarily beautiful men and women, before whose charms none can resist: in our folklore, the incubus and succubus. Rofomagus talks of these, identifying them as demons of a particular sort.

Those spirits which men call the *succubus* and *incubus* are unimportant minions among the legions of Hell; they do not even have names. Their power over men and women is most strong though; none except those protected by magic can resist their corrupting influence.

To summon these spirits is a simple matter. The magus must prepare and burn a mixture containing juniper berries, sandalwood, musk oil, mistletoe and the sexual secretions of a man (if the spirit is to be an incubus) or woman (if the succubus is to appear). A simple incantation will then cause the desired creature to appear. Except for the eyes, which have the likeness of black abysses filled with flickering lights, they appear entirely human, and of flawless beauty.

The creature must be given a lock of hair from the head of the person whose debauchment is to be accomplished. It will then vanish, reappearing in a spot where a meeting may be effected. An incubus will return afterwards and generally will have become very bad-tempered and may utter vile language, for it detests humans. It may then be dismissed.

If the creature is summoned as a succubus it will remain longer, for it cannot abide to have human semen within its body. It will transform itself into an incubus and find the first female it can to seduce, thus ridding itself of its unwanted burden. Such a union will invariably prove fertile, but the child is most often stillborn. If it is born alive and grows to adulthood it will have the mark of the demon upon it, and will become licentious, dissolute and violent, and will most often end its life on the gallows.

CHAPTER FOUR

ALCHEMIST AND OCCULTIST

Alchemy

While the bulk of the Ruckhurst Manuscript is concerned with the researches of Rofomagus, master magician, a portion of it is devoted to the work of Geoffrey Carlyle, the scholarly and respectable occultist who was the face presented by Rofomagus to the outside world. Here we read of his experiments in alchemy, his dealings with astrology and with prophecy, and his observations on the growth of witchcraft and witch persecution. Alchemical research was widespread in the sixteenth century, though falling into disfavour in many countries. Carlyle's writings suggest that he was able to succeed where many others had failed.

Through my researches I have gained respect and scorn in equal measure among scholars of my acquaintance. My study of this science has been much assisted by my mastery of the Art, for whereas other alchemists must depend on partial and corrupt histories on which to base their researches, I have been able through the intercession of Astaroth to view directly those moments of discovery. I have seen the lost tomb of Hermes Trismegistus and read from the emerald tablet held in his mummified hand the words which set forth the basic tenets of the alchemist's beliefs:

> T'is true, without falsehood and most real: that which is above is like that which is below, to perpetrate the miracles of one thing. And as all things have been derived from one, by the thought of one, so all things are born from this thing, by adoption. The sun is its father, the moon is its mother.

Wind has carried it in its belly, the earth is its nurse. Here is the father of every perfection in the world. His strength and power are absolute when changed into earth; thou wilt separate the earth from fire, the subtle from the gross, gently and with care. It ascends from earth to heaven, and descends again to earth to receive the power of the superior and the inferior things. By this means, thou wilt have the glory of the world. And because of this, all obscurity will flee from thee. Within this is the power, most powerful of all powers. For it will overcome all subtle things, and penetrate every solid thing. Thus the world was created. From this will be, and will emerge, admirable adaptations of which the means are here. And for this reason I am called Hermes Trismegistus, having the three parts of the philosophy of the world. What I have said of the sun's operations is accomplished.

Practitioners of the hermetic arts suppose the import of this to be that all metals are composed from sulphur and mercury, and may be derived from these two substances mixed in different proportions. Sulphur and mercury are the seeds from which all metals may be grown, as the acorn is the seed from which comes the oak tree. I sense that this is but a partial truth, and that the proper explanation is that sulphur and mercury themselves, like other metals and indeed like all corporeal things, are composed of other, smaller seeds whose nature we do not comprehend. If it were possible to find and mix these seeds, then any substance might be transmuted into any other, and great power would be in the hands of men.

For the purpose of turning base metal into gold, which is the goal of all alchemists no matter how philosophical they state their purpose to be, an agent is necessary, this being the substance which has been termed the Philosopher's Stone. Some claim to have seen it and used it; others, far fewer in number, know how it is to be made. This knowledge was imparted to me by Agrippa, most learned of alchemical researchers, and involves a lengthy combustion of a most complex mixture of substances in the heat of the alchemical furnace.

The Stone, when it appears, has the appearance of a viscous dark red liquid, which congeals into a substance not unlike a large crystal of quartz. It is quite fragile, and may readily be broken into smaller fragments. Its potency is great; a single crumb will suffice for many operations, for the Stone is not itself consumed in the reaction. The methods suggested for performing the transmutation of base metal into gold with the aid of the Stone are many, but in reality the operation is quite simple and depends on the mere proximity of the elements. I have found it quite sufficient simply to envelop the stone in virgin wax, then slowly drip mercury or molten lead on to it. As the droplets of metal pass around the stone, they are transformed into gold of the purest quality.

This gold is of great value to the magus, for it is virgin metal, which greatly increases in potency any spell in which it is used. If prepared for this purpose it must be made and used on the same day as or the days immediately preceding an operation.

The practice of this transformation should not be publicly performed, for gold arouses great greed in all men, and he who proves himself able to manufacture it cannot expect gentle treatment at the hands of those consumed by the desire to possess it. Many is the vain braggart who has ended his life on the rack or the wheel, seeking to deny the knowledge he had previously, and falsely, claimed to have. I have no need of wealth, and am content by this means to manufacture such gold as I require for my experiments; fellow alchemists and sceptics alike know me as yet another dedicated but unsuccessful researcher.

Nostradamus

On the nature of prophecy I have been much intrigued by the accounts of Michel de Notre Dame, known as Nostradamus, who is my guest in this year of 1556. I must ignore his urgent entreaty that none of what he tells me should be committed to writing. He is much concerned for his safety, being decried as 'witch' in certain quarters of France, although he has found favour with divers Royals, whose concern for power leads them to consult with astrologers.

Nostradamus is a practitioner of much achievement, and from him I have hoped to become an adept of far-seeing, sufficient that I may practice at the courts of England, and win favour for myself as a scholar. My own evocation of Astaroth, which rewards me with liaison to the past, does not allow such forward vision. Nostradamus invokes no major demon in the means he has perfected for envisioning the times of the World until the end of Man. Before Armageddon's fire consumes it he sees not five centuries more. In all of those remaining epochs he sees a time of great conflict, the rise and fall of Common Men of Power. In fields, he envisages the bloody armies of nations, men in number greater than the stars, their weapons spitting death like iron cobras. I have witnessed these visions with him and verify their awesome appearance.

He has educated me thoroughly in the manner of conjuring these visions. Essential is an iron dish, shallow in the centre, beaten across a mould of iron-chiselled stone. The inner surface of this dish must be blackened before each prophetic search by the burning of pitchblende and a mixture of belladonna and the dark earth from below a deep-rooted stone. Water from a well, taken during the hour and on the day of Mercury (for the planet Mercury governs knowledge and the seeing of the future) is placed in the dish, which is mounted on a tripod.

To witness a vision of a Man of Power he marks his hands with the four signs of fire, and counts forward in years from the present time, until he reaches the time of his study. Walking five times widdershins around the dish, his hands across the still water, he invokes the angels MICHAEL and RAPHAEL, and adjures the spirits of Oak and Earth to cast their shadows through the ages and bring back the vision. Finally he dabs water from the dish upon his ears, eyes, lips and nose and thus shuts off his senses from the present. In the still water he looks forward, the vision resolving across the inner surface of the dish.

I have consulted with Nostradamus concerning my own future and he has seen the moment of my greatest power. Some dark event is foreshadowed there and he described the vision in a riddle:

> The boy from the country
> Cannot control the man of power.
> One of the three brothers
> Is not confined by the cage.

The Secret Arts

Two hundred and fifty years after Geoffrey Carlyle's death, the French occultist Eliphas Levi (Alphonse-Louis Constant) wrote: 'To attain the *sanctum regum*, that is, the knowledge and power of the magi, there are four indispensible conditions – an intelligence illuminated by study, an intrepidity which nothing can check, a will which nothing can break, and a discretion which nothing can corrupt and nothing intoxicate. TO KNOW, TO DARE, TO WILL, TO KEEP SILENCE...'

It is a fact, both uncanny and stimulating, that this passage appears *word for word* (in English) in one of the manuscripts discovered in the workshop of Rofomagus. Was Geoffrey Carlyle merely recording the words of another occultist, to whose work Levi would later have access? Or can it be that some of Carlyle's manuscript papers *were* known before the discoveries of 1977?

In his journal, the passage appears during a discussion on the difficulties of the practitioners of the Secret Arts in retaining an acceptable public face.

To keep silence is best served by the deliberate public practice of those arts that are commonly and widely in demand, namely astrology, physiognomy, cheiromancy, the art of memory, geomancy, and the like. No-one questions the man who can use his arcane knowledge to lead to favourable inclinations being read from palm, face, skull, stars and so forth. In truth, there are many charlatans at work using some slight knowledge of these sciences to earn reputations as diviners of the future. They depend on the common belief that the future is pre-ordained, a belief so widespread among the Christian faithful that there seems little point in denying it to those who come for consultation. It is clear to those of the Enneas, however, that the future is fragile, and is neither fixed nor certain. The study of planetary motion is certainly of great utility in determining the most favourable times for a ceremony to be conducted, but cannot truly be applied to the nature of one man's destiny.

What of Nostradamus's predictions? Did Carlyle take them literally? It seems unlikely, for the quatrain produced for Carlyle himself clearly indicates that the magician would fail in his efforts to perform the 'ultimate summoning', and yet Carlyle went ahead. He writes:

To know the way the future is planned is to enable those of cunning mind, and adept in the ways of power, to alter the shape of that future. By symbol and secret name, so can great truths be bent to minor whim.

As a student of the *Doctrine of Correspondences*, a work attributed to Hermes Trismegistus, Rofomagus would have been deeply concerned with how the material universe could be affected by ritual, and how the material universe of *past and future* could be likewise affected. The doctrine states simply that all material things reflect a cosmic principle, and that principle may be addressed by *symbols* (talismans, seals, words and names of power). When the symbol is manipulated, that which it reflects is manipulated also. As above, so below; time present, time past, time future.

If Rofomagus was scornful of astrology, however, he was at least convinced of the relation between the stars and ritual. For example, he lists the familiar associations between the Zodiac and the parts of the body, with Aries affecting the face and neck, Gemini the shoulders and arms, Cancer affecting the lungs, chest and breasts, Leo the heart and stomach, Libra the navel, loins, buttocks and kidneys, Scorpio the genitalia and so on. Thus, in a ceremony using heart blood, or one designed to affect the heart, the sign of Leo would be most important: plants would be cut when the Moon was in Leo, instruments prepared during times of the Sun etc.

With regard to reading the lines on the palms of the hand and the face, Rofomagus, after describing the procedure, adds only this:

Work and the weariness of life become marked upon the skin. By this means can the magus concentrate upon the life of the man or woman being addressed and divine their weaknesses, and wishes. By touching and concentrating upon hand or face, a deep insight may be gained through inner vision, and this may be effectively translated into the lines on the hand or forehead. These practices are children's games for charlatans; to the true magus the lines mean nothing, but are a focus for his probing mind.

Finally, on numbers (the modern numerology) Rofomagus is equally scathing.

There are those who seek even beyond the secret names of power for the numbers that lie at their root. This *reducto ad absurdum* has at times proved useful as a disguise, for the number of my own name is that of a dull, plodding man, and in the past I have been ignored by Inquisitors for that very reason. What foolish belief! The numbers have power only when used in conjunction with both names and the elemental substances associated with the force to be invoked.

Covens and Witch Burning

In his role as an intellectual, functioning in open society, Geoffrey Carlyle would have been very wary of any association with witches, especially those he refers to as *malefica*, the contemporary name for black, or evil witches. Throughout Europe, by Carlyle's time, witches were commonly executed, by hanging, burning or flaying alive, and the Witchfinder — usually a Churchman — was an infrequent, but already very sinister phenomenon in the country. Whole communities could be turned from what Carlyle calls the *religio paganorum*, that is, the religion of the country people, into fervent witch haters. Even as an astrologist Carlyle ran the risk of falling foul of the Church and being declared a 'witch'. Naturally, he would have guarded all knowledge of the Enneas, the Secret Cabal, with spells and great fervour.

In this ancient place [Ruckhurst] there is much secret practice of the *religio paganorum*, a worship of deities and demons common among the country peoples of all parts of these Isles. The Church has outlawed such worship, seeing in all pagan practice that particular adoration reserved for the *malefica*: the adoration of Satan and his host. Of true witches in this area I know of only five; three are wise women, who have inherited their powers and position from others; they are adept at healing, at preparing concoctions of minor magic use, and they possess some small talent for clairvoyance. They are tolerated by those of a strong Christian belief, but are made unwelcome by them. But hounded and much harassed by the Church are those two witches who can be called black; they are evil women, and shape-changers, and have inflicted much harm upon the community out of nought but simple spite. Towards these I direct restraining spells, but I am aware of their links with others of their kind, and I fear to draw down the power of true evil upon the communities nearby. The problem can be resolved in only one way, which is to say, with the touch of fire.

The simple practice of a simple magic among the country folk owes much to a tradition as ancient as my own, and I have studied their rituals with interest. They celebrate feasts at four times of the year, and sometimes more, and these major feasts are linked to the new seasons. Part of their worship is towards the Moon Goddess, who is known as Diana, or Hecate, or Selene. Hecate rules dogs, ghosts, tombs and crossroads, and these night feasts are invariably celebrated at the crossroads near Drustone Wood, where the rotten trunk of an oak has been used as a gibbet for this past century or more. Here, too, can be found the ruins of an early church, sacked (it is said) by Norsemen at the time of Alfred. I have heard the community call upon Aethelburt, who was the first priest here, and the spirit has risen at their command to assist them with their worship.

During those feasts that make obeisance to the Powers of Darkness, I have seen much elevating of the body by use of a simple spell and a powerful pomade. This ointment can be made in various ways, but the most effective is by mixing aconite and belladonna with hellbore root, hemlock and bat's blood, all gathered in the appropriate hour. This is thickened to an ointment with soot that is mixed with the blood of a human infant taken (without killing) in the hour of Mercury, on the day of the Moon. This is spread upon the skin and upon the instrument of flying, be it stick, or sword, or broom, and by invoking a minor demon the body may then move about the area of the ceremony, but may not cross still water.

Those evil women who are *malefica* most often disguise themselves as screech owls, but I have seen them move by magic, and by use of such a philtre as can cause elevation of the body. They cannot cross water, nor a line between two churches or pagan tombs that are in sight of each other. But there is a power in the Earth along such lines and there are those, adept at magic, who can use that power.

Those feasts that are celebrated at the times of the old druidic seasons are attended by men, women and children all, and they are drawn from miles around. The Church has seen fit, these last years, to refer to such revelry as a *sabbat*. In this way they link paganism with twisted religion, which justifies their attempt to hound 'witches' and 'satanic worship' from the countryside. In truth, the communities hereabouts are strong adherents to that principle of duality that caused the Knights of the Temple to be destroyed (although they know of the duality of God through instinct rather than teaching), and they thus celebrate the ruler of Heaven and his angels as much as they celebrate the ruler of Earth, and those angels who have fallen. They do not refer to Satan by name, nor do they summon demons (contrary to what the Church would imply). They invoke, at various times, both God and Diana, and in their festive prayer is clear evidence that all such feasts are a celebration of the three-fold nature of a Mother Protector, or Goddess: the youthful Luna; the lover of life and men who is Diana; and the ageing haunter of the underworld, Proserpine. The 'priest', who is clad as the idol of worship, is a woman, full figured and strong, who takes upon her body the cold, erect phallus of a male Deity, and the mask of a ram. Thus she is a symbol of all that is High and all that is Low, of the conjuction of the two sexes, of the animal that is in man, and of the godhead that is in animals.

At these simple *sabbats* all present go either naked, which in summer is preferred, or clad in the skins and masks of the animals of the land: as horses, cows, wolves, owls, cats, bats, frogs, sometimes goats. They dance from right to left, holding hands, and moving with exaggerated slowness. Such sinister motion is of great offence to the Church. Sometimes they dance back to back, again in opposition to the accepted Christian tradition. All of these things, and the sexual freedom that accompanies feasting in Spring and Summer, are seen as Devil Worship, but they are more truly a tradition of the ancient country, and celebrate the Earth, and Heaven, and the bountiful harvest of the soil, and of woman, and of a joy in nature that has vanished from Holy Consciousness.

Then there are those *sabbats* wherein *malefica* make attendance, that is, those black witches whose vile hold upon a community can often be mortal.

At these the area of worship is marked out with the skulls of horse, cow and human, preferably from animals and men that have been slaughtered in the full vigour of life. The fire is used not just for warmth but to roast, for consumption, the grisly remains of an infant sacrifice. Such *malefica*, who conduct the *sabbat*, and who cast spells of stupefaction over those ordinary people who attend upon the feast, invariably have made pacts in blood with minor demons, and summon their Masters using incantation and sacrifice. The demons appear as black dogs, although they are sometimes seen as hideously malformed men, or cats, or goats. The dog accomplishes sexual union with the *malefica*, and the semen is collected and is of great power in the working of evil.

References to witchcraft, and in particular to the 'wise' and 'black' witches operating in the environs of Ruckhurst, appear frequently in those manuscript pages of Carlyle's journal that seem to have been written towards the end of his life. Carlyle functioned in society as an astrologer, astronomer, practitioner of herbal arts, and all the rest of the 'acceptable' face of alchemy. Visitors to his house were frequent, often young and in need of advice on love or fortune, and Geoffrey Carlyle was content to both attend at Church, and to defend, in society, the 'wise women' of the community, the witches who were not malevolent. Thus it was with considerable anger that he made this note in the manuscript, in mirror writing, and in his own blood mixed with ink:

Fie! And the Fury of Hell on John Cotteswood! Damnation to the Church where John Cotteswood is priest. In the black name of ASMODEUS, AZAZEL and BAAL and in the Holy Name of the archangel TZAPHQIEL, wasting and malignancy to Margaret Becquet, black witch and foul fiend of night and the dead earth. SHAMAD, SHAMAD, ASHMA, BAZTAOTH, QADOSCH, SHAMAD.*

Peace and the Eternity of God's Pleasure to Isobel Markham, taken this day and burned without true trial, through the spell and deception of Margaret Becquet, who made her own face upon the Innocent, and sent her to the flames in her place. The Fire revealed the truth, and in her death the Innocent cursed the *Malefica*. May that curse find the favour of God in the Holy Names of ALEPH, DELOTH, NIN, IOD.

*Editor's Note: SHAMAD and QADOSCH are Hebrew for Destroy and Holy respectively. BAZTAOTH is obscure.

CHAPTER FIVE

LOVE SPELLS
AND
OTHER SPELLS

Love Spells

Those pages of Rofomagus' manuscripts that constitute his grimoire, or spell book, are untidy, confused, and crammed with details. Many of the spells which he records are clearly incomplete, in the area of detail that, say, a modern cook might think unnecessary to record (the actual volume of a teaspoon, or the precise weight constituted by a 'pinch' of salt). The spells are mostly of a trivial nature, essential, however, for concocting effective summonings, or actions at a distance. The first spell in the sheets is, 'On the subduing of the demon inhabitant of mandrake'; the second, 'To elevate fever and cause burning'. The most elaborate rituals are those related to necromancy, to the summoning of the demon Astaroth (see elsewhere) and of course to the summoning and control of Major Demons. He made a study of cursing, death spells, love spells and spells for inducing various causes and effects in man, animal and indeed in nature, across a wide distance. Clearly, from notes found elsewhere, Rofomagus was much in demand as a purveyor of love potions and philtres, and advice on winning hearts.

A more complete grimoire will be published in due course, when all the coded sequences have been deciphered, and when a decision has been made on the advisability of publishing spells in such a complete form.

For a girl whose monthly flow is strong and who is powerfully influenced by the moon, this method of bestirring love in a man is best: at dusk, within hearing of a nightingale, she should cavort naked in the mud and litter of a stream or river bank until she is thoroughly grimed, thence return to home and cleanse her body in water of almost intolerable heat. The steam and moisture that will ensure from her pores thereafter is absorbed with flour, and from this dough, mixed with powdered cuttings from her fingers, toes and bodily hair, a cake is baked. Whichever male shall then eat this cake will have love only for the girl.

Rofomagus makes a bitter addition to this spell:

In order to avenge a love slighted, bake the cake with sweat and excretion from a young heifer, and mix with powdered animal hair and hoof clippings. The faithless man fed this vengeful mix will romantically persue the heifer until his heart breaks

For a man who has affinity with the sun, but who can induce calm in horses and is favoured by Epona, moon goddess, this manner of spell to win a girl's favour: take a length of thin braid, in which is entwined even a single hair of the girl N. Tie seven knots along its length, saying, 'This knot is thy eye, N., which is closed to me; this knot is thy mouth, N., which is closed to me', and so on for all the apertures of the body. It will be necessary for the girl to step across the braid unknowingly. Then, on each day following the New Moon, unravel one knot

saying, 'This is thy eye, N., which through Diana, Hecate, Demeter and with the indulgence of Asmodeus, sees only me; this is thy mouth...which speaks only of me', and so on for each aperture of the body, stating what is required of each. The seventh knot is for the heart. Beware: the unravelling of charmed knots is a dangerous and powerful means to gain control and inflict hurt, and it must be used with care. Care must also taken in the order of unravelling, for the nature of the love will be ordered by preference.

This way for a girl to know the name of her future lover: pin each possible name to the bulb of an onion, gathered on June 12th, and pricked with a tear. Place the bulbs in a copper box. Inspect every day and the love of he who will be truest will cause that bulb to sprout. Another method is to collect snails from the garden on the night that follows the fullest face of the moon and place in a copper box with a drop of thy blood. Overnight the creatures will form trails of slime, and those marked with colour will form the initials of thy lover to be.

To know his face, sit at a mirror on the night of the New Moon; the mirror should face a window, illuminated by two white candles. Make out of dough the shape of a man, and squeeze upon it the juice of the yellow berry of mandrake (but do not gather this without assistance, for the mandrake is potent and dangerous in its magic). Drink a bitter brew of endive, purslain, valerian, jasmine, crocus, coriander, fern and pansy. At the hour of midnight place the figurine across thy heart and say, staring into the mirror, 'SATOR, AREPO, TENET, OPERA, ROTAS, IAH, IAH, ENAM, SHADRACH, MESCHACH, ABEDNEGO, Out of thy loveless sleep arise and show thyself to me, and be not harmed by thy passage, in the name of HANIEL, ANAEL, GABRIEL.'

In the reflection of the window the wraith of thy lover will appear.

Rofomagus was terrified of invisibility, and invisible vengeance, and his three spells on the subject, 'How to render thyself invisible', are half written in code, annotated with warnings, and deliberately confused. One of them, the most powerful and effective, he had clearly learned from the Keys of Solomon:

Make a small image of a man in yellow wax; do this in the month of January, in the day and the hour of Saturn. Slice off the top of the head and inscribe upon the wax this character: [see diagram]. Replace the head and seal it to the figure. Now write on the dried skin of a frog or toad this character, [see diagram] and tie the skin about the figure.

Suspend the figure in a dark place, a cavern, or secret lair, using thy own hair as the rope; do this at midnight, and perfume the figure with an incense of dragonfly wing, aloes wood, fern and the perfumed dew from a spider's web, slung between the branches of hawthorn. Now say, 'METATRON, MELEKH, BE-ROTH, NOTH, VENIBBETH, MACH and all ye I conjure thee, oh figure of wax, by the living God that by virtue of these characters and words thou render me invisible wherever I may bear thee with me, Amen.' After having censed it anew, bury the figure in a small deal box, and cover with fresh earth. Whenever invisibility is required, carry the figure on the left side of the body; bury it anew when its use is done.

Beware invisibility for it drains the life essence, and renders thee susceptible to demons. Great is the passage of time in the state of invisibility, and for the incautious a century may pass in but a week.

Curses and Transformation Spell

Rofomagus' grimoire is littered with curses and spells of the sort that we would call 'psychic attack', that is, the projection of evil intent — usually fatal — in the form of either suggestibility, or an intangible figure, invisible to all but the victim. Rofomagus devised many killing spells himself, but also has adapted the sympathetic magic of pre-medieval times to great effect. He writes that 'malediction is of particular precise application; each malign discourse must depend on knowing the subject. Very little is required in order to know the victim well enough for the malediction to be effective, but tears are better than hair if they can be collected.'

His grimoire lists numerous alchemical processes whereby different bodily exudates or clippings should be analysed to determine the direction of the curse that will be placed upon their unwitting donor. Tears, for example, should be treated with a dilution of sulphur and the juice of ragwort, mixed to a paste with moss gathered from the eastern side of an elm tree. This is smeared upon the breast of a cat, which will make noises appropriate to the type of curse needed. Nail clippings should be chewed for one hour with a mixture of nightbane and beeswax, and a dough in which a drop of bird lime has been baked. By this daunting process a vision of the correct words will appear to the magus.

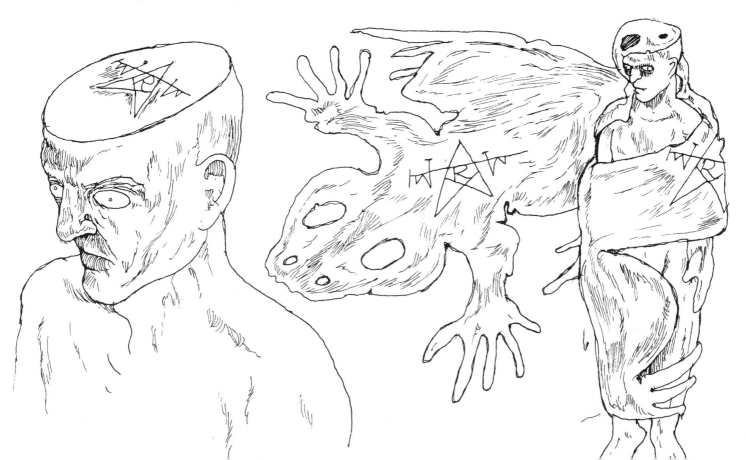

In the matter of cursing the Irish are greatly skilled, though they are notorious for their wanton exaggeration of the process. In the south of that vile and cheerless land I have witnessed the laying of a curse upon Conall, Lord of Rathgar, performed by the Irish mage Lethlobar son of Cathal. First he fasted for seven days and nights, seated at the edge of Rathgar's land, in sight of the house and stables. In this way he concentrated his mind, and the agony of his body, towards the man to be maligned. At the conclusion of the fast Lethlobar stood upon a low hill with six men who were known to him, three of them of the Holy Orders. Here they planted a severed blackthorn branch, and stood in a ring about it, facing outwards, Lethlobar staring at the house of the cursed Lord. When the wind blew from the north (which eventuality required a freezing wait of three hours) they passed a perforated stone about the ring from right to left, and held the point of a thorn into their thumbs, drawing blood. Lehlobar uttered the curse in the following form:

> Evil! Death! Short agony of life to the Lord of Rathgar!
> May the horns of a dun bull destroy Rathgar!
> May the biting winds of winter cause a flood of water in Rathgar's chest!
> May each mouthful of food that Rathgar eats cause him pain and poison!
> May Rathgar's limbs waste, his sex deplete, his wit vanish to the four winds!
> May Rathgar perish in misery and alone, may Rathgar pay in hell!
> Under rocks and mounds, digested by worms, may Rathgar be!*

Rofomagus placed great store by one cursing ritual he observed, also in Ireland:

To perform a wish of ill health, bad luck, or lingering death, the name of the cursed is scratched upon five round pebbles, which are placed on a blackthorn fire. Kneeling before the fire, the curse is uttered for an hour or more, the body rocking forward, the voice raised in passion and fury. In the wishing of ill luck upon a man, this is the order of words: 'By the powerful Creator, and the Holy Virgin, may the blight take every one of your crops and lay waste to your hand; by the Saints and Angels may your eyes burn and your manhood turn to flax; may there not be a day when you do not stumble in your walk; may rain fall on you and wind blow through you; may your wife be taken by an Englishman; may your children, and their children, and their children in turn all speak with the burbling of idiocy. May all this happen until these stones go on fire'.

The words thus spoken, the stones are hidden individually in all corners of the land. This is a powerful curse, and I have witnessed its success, applied to a man called Donne.

---

*Editor's note: in the accounts of the Parish of Dundalk for 1550, reference is made to the death of Conall, Lord of Rathgar, mauled by a bull 'which thus ended the pauperish life of this afflicted man'.

One the strongest, and most unusual, of curses was that which caused the transformation of man into beast. Whilst those who were practised in the occult and so-called Black Arts could shape-change easily, for the common man to be so afflicted was an abhorrent, and deeply feared imprisonment. Rofomagus called such spells 'grim deeds', and lists a number of ways in which men may be transformed into goats, crows, cats and even lowlier animals. He also records the means of reversal in the most unusual case of all.

He that has been cursed into the shape, form and existence of a frog or toad is almost beyond help, for the malediction has been induced with the aid of the demon Belial, the Worthless One, who will have taken of the life of the maldoer [he who lays the curse] and thus marked the spell as powerful and binding.

He who is thus cursed will have been induced, without his knowledge, to consume the spawn of a frog that has been seeped with the juice of hellbore, mixed with semen collected after copulation with a beast, and fouled with the blood of worms, slugs and other creatures of the low earth. A frog, much decayed, is impaled with two iron nails, and this object left on the hearth of the cursed man. When he discovers it he will not touch it, but the animus of a lower beast will begin to haunt him, and slowly possess him. Say these words if you would practice this evil spell, and say them at dawn, by a pond that is filled with spawn, and facing in the direction of the cursed man's house: 'ENDOM, FANTAGRABIS, AMPHIBIS, TERTACH, MORACH, BEELBEGG, all ye who squirm, and worm, all ye who slither and slime, all ye of the low earth, who croak, grunt and crawl, take unto thy number N., who is toad in the shape of man, and make him man in the shape of toad.'

Over the next few days he will take to his bed, and begin to shrivel, shrink, twist and transform.

To reverse the transformation it will be necessary to find a girl of royal birth, who is intact and who has never known true love. She should be of a birth sign of Earth, yet with Venus rising in Leo on the day of her birth, and the Moon in Libra. She should be influenced by the Moon in her passions, and be of a gentle disposition. Instruct this girl to eat honey scented with John's wort and mixed with sweat and breast milk from a young couple in true love; instruct her then to drink a concoction of dandelion, lily and the urine of a female frog, collected during spawning. This drink may be sweetly flavoured to avoid repugnance. At dusk, twenty four hours later and when the moon is quite full, the girl must kiss, lick and cover with the soft juices of her mouth the transformed creature, and do so without repulsion, or nausea, and do so with love, so that the juices of her mouth are magically charged with scents and signals of femaleness. If this is done in detail, then within a week the frog will turn back into the man.

Death Spells

Carlyle's association with the mysterious cabal, the Enneas, required him (for reasons unspecified) to be adept in the act of transmitting harm, and death, to another, by magic means whether sympathetic or spell-induced. He describes the creating of a 'fetch', a soulless, malignant elemental, of manlike yet hideous appearance and visible only to the victim, which could cause the strangulation or evisceration of that victim. To produce such a fetch, a ceremony of Mars is used, with iron implements, and an iron sword for a wand, the magus dressed in red, and invoking Asmodeus, demon of the fifth sephira, the house of Mars. Most potent in all magical rituals involving blood, especially in those designed, like the fetch, to transmit harm, fear or anxiety, is blood taken from a man executed in full health, this blood being charged with vigour and made potent with the man's bitter resentment.

These are the ways of killing, at a distance from the victim's house, and by the infernal intervention of dark spirits:

Take soil from four places around the victim's house; mix with a paste of oak leaf, rotted bark and fresh mandrake, taken from the ground by a black dog.

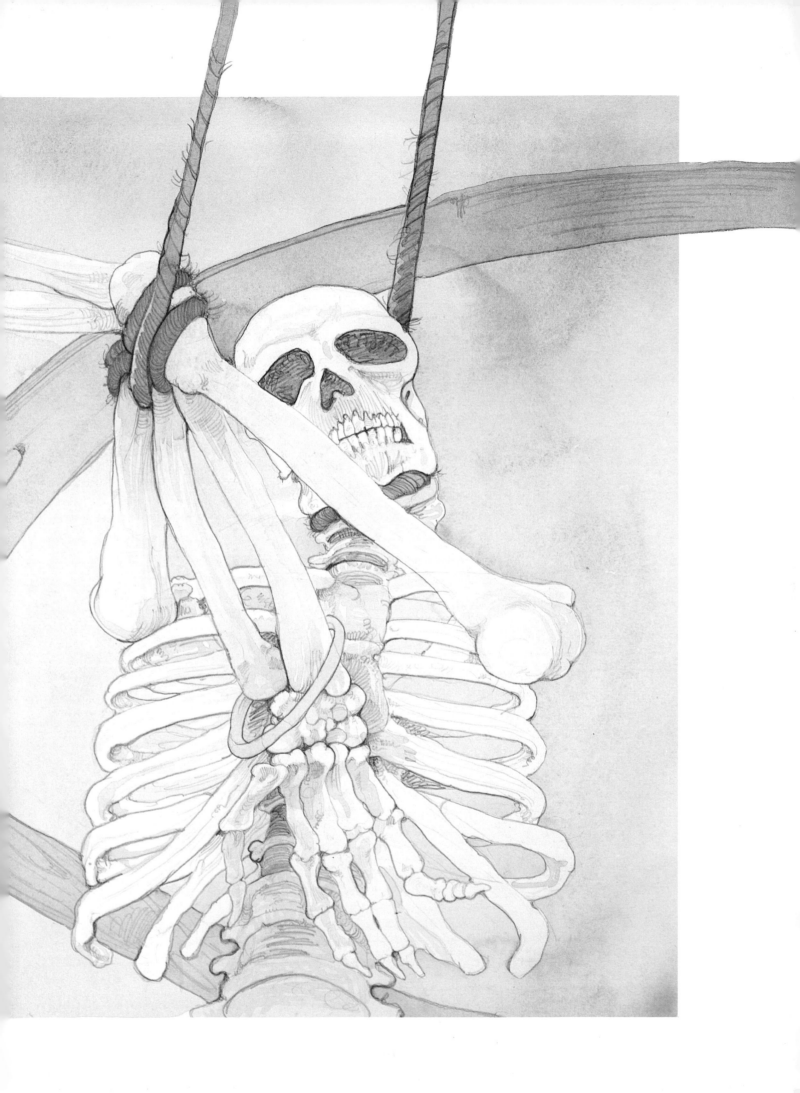

Add resin and knead until the clay is thick; shape into a human form and impress upon the shape the holes in the body, and the eyes and fingers; bind to the body some part of the victim that has been attained by devious means; nails, hair, clothing, tears or urine. Do with this mannequin exactly what you will, saying, 'In the name of Persephone, in the name of Hermes, may evil pass between me and N., may the limbs of N. burn without flame, may his body cease to pass excrement, may the poison of my evil cause his heart to stop.'

Take an animal of lesser nature, preferably a toad or similar beast. Baptise it with water from a font, solemnly and properly with the name of the intended victim. Say, 'In the name of the Holy Ghost, the Son and the Father, and their infernal enemies, I baptise thee N. May Hecate bind thee limb to limb and wit to wit.' Thus baptised, the beast may be tortured, twisted and killed, and this will be seen to be done to the victim.

Take an iron blade that has rusted, and immerse this in a mixture of blood and excrement from a cat, dog or similar small animal kept caged. When the mixture is dry carve the name of the victim on the blade, on both sides. Carry this blade across the heart for seven days and seven nights, and never cease to think of the victim, saying, 'This blade to thy heart, this poison to thy blood, the death of the animal to thy death'. At dawn of the eighth day slaughter the caged beast with the iron blade, saying, 'As thy blood drains, so life drains. In the Name of the Princes of Darkness, and of Hecate, and the Lord of Animals, I wish away thy life.'

Obtain by devious means: a fragment of the victim's clothing and shape this into a human form; fingernails and hair, stitch these onto the cloth; tears or other excrement, daub upon the cloth. Tie the cloth mannequin into a pouch of white linen, and tie the pouch with your own hair. Impale the pouch with splinters of wood or sharpened bone, and at each point of entry paint the symbol of a demon, saying, 'Into this cavity I wish the dead spirit of (name the demon) to draw out thy life; through this split in thy spirit I wish thy blood to drain.' To trap the spirit of the victim, tie the pouch to the upmost branches of an oak, saying, 'Until this oak dies, thy spirit is bound here.'

Take a strip of hide, cleaned and dried, and preferably of a calf slaughtered during the dark night of winter. Mark the inner surface of the skin with the name of the victim, and cut the name with an iron knife. Carve or daub the horned symbol of the Lord of Beasts, thrice, around the name, saying, 'From the Earth, from the Woodland, may the Horned Lord of Darkness take thy life for fodder. May the Hunter spear thy body and thy spirit with his horned blade.'

But beware, for the spirit that is invoked to take the life of the victim is a hunter of the ancient world, a potent force of nature, and will as easily take the evildoer as the victim. Listen for the sound of hounds, and the stampede of wild horses; protect yourself with the symbol of Venus painted upon the skull of a stag, and the Hunter will pass you by.

Obtain the skull of a cat, or rat, or dog that has been corroded in the Earth. Paint the features of the victim upon the skull in red or brown ochre. Use the sharpened long bones of a tiny mammal to impale the ears and eyes or the skull, pushing through to the cavity of the brain. Hide the skull at a place where the victim lives, or works, or frequents. Madness will ensure within nine days. Death may then be achieved by retrieving the skull and contriving for the victim to crush it.

Sever the left hand of a corpse that is no more than seven days dead; that of a hanged man is preferable to that of a man dead by beheading, but the corpse must have died by violence. It is possible that if the corpse is less than a day dead by natural means, the necessary attributes may be instilled into the stolen member by strangling the body with a flaxen rope. Squeeze the severed hand until all blood is gone. Heat the hand, without burning, and collect the fat that drips. Immerse the hand in vinegar and reunite it with the blood, and with the juice of hemlock, henbane and mandrake. After seven full days, unite the hand with your own blood and urine, excreted whilst invoking the name of the demon whose power will be used through the hand. Make a candle from wax, mixed with fat from the hand, and use this to char the hand whenever it is to be used for evil purpose. Bend the fingers of the hand such that the small and first finger appear as the horns of the Hunter. This awesome member will silence lips, induce deep sleep, and may be utilised to strangle sleeping men. It is a formidable tool and will easily turn against the owner, so safeguards must be made.

Necromancy

Although in its modern context, the art of necromancy has come to mean specifically a divination of the future using the corpse of someone newly dead, re-united with its spirit, in Rofomagus' time it was an art of wider scope, utilising pieces of the dead, or ghosts, or restless spirits to both divine the future and to locate hidden treasure. (This latter practice was particularly perilous since buried treasure was protected by forces linked to the Sun, and were thus in direct opposition to the Lunar and Saturnine forces that controlled the raising of the dead). Nevertheless, the most powerful practice of the necromancer was the re-instating of spirit with corpse, and the animation of the corpse, by which process:

...the soul, restless and still bound to earth, will perceive the shadow world beyond our own, and may be compelled to reveal its vision, or knowledge, in the name of Mercury. But this is a dangerous practice, for it conjures forces of great evil, misery, discord and injury in the name of the Lord of Death [Saturn] and attracts them to the necromancer himself.

On any consecrated ground — such as a graveyard — guardian spirits attend to the protection of the site. The spirit of the last corpse buried in a cemetary remains attached to the place, guarding it against minor demons, until its role is taken by a newer arrival. Such a spirit is useless for necromantic purposes (it has no vision of the higher plane) but must be protected against; this, in Rofomagus' words, is:

...something I have often witnessed causing the death of the necromancer. To be insufficiently prepared is to court death of a most appalling kind, for these guardian spirits can strangle and cause evisceration, and will defy both invocations to the Holy Trinity and to the Prince of Darkness. Few practitioners of our magic art know of the full ritual that must be undertaken in the raising of spirit and corpse from the fresh earth; charlatans and hoaxers have devised elaborate procedures, involving animal sacrifices and chanting that is impressive, but serves only to anger the servants of Hell. From my colleague John Dee I have learned the mathematical game that must be played in order to keep those lesser elementals at bay which might otherwise penetrate the protective circle, they

not being bound in the same fashion as the Princes of Hell. But Dee, alas, is duped by charlatans, whose vision in the scrying glass is mere fancy and induced by inhaling the dream-inducing fumes of certain mushrooms, and designed to win favour from the Queen, and from Dee himself.*[see Note]

To consult with a corpse of not more than one month in the clay the preparation involves an abstinence of nine days in this fashion: no sight of woman or child, nor sound of their voices; contemplation of Hecate, the dweller in the Void, who is demon (some would say Goddess) of ghosts, death and sterility; it is essential that the necromancer dresses in stinking grave clothes and sleeps on the purloined lid of a rotting oak coffin; each dawn and dusk, and in each hour of Saturn during the day and night, the body must be washed in wormy earth, taken from a grave more than 99 years old; the bowels should be darkly cleansed with the same earth, and the excrement so produced later used in the marking of the circle around the grave; food should be restricted to the cooked flesh of dogs, to black bread without leaven and salt, and to grape juice without ferment, all consumed from vessels of lead. Thus sustained on victuals that are empty of that which may prevent putrefaction after death, and of the spirit of life, matter without spirit, a communion is established between sorcerer and death. During these nine days the funeral service should be recited at dawn and at dusk, but always after washing; the necromancer should spend all other time lying in the position of a corpse, hands crossed on chest.

At the first hour of Saturn of the new day, which is to say, after sunset, burn henbane, hemlock, aloes wood, opium and saffron on the grave to be opened. When it is safe to continue without the prying eyes of other men, protect against the guardian of the cemetary by tying a cat, made ill with hemlock and given the name NECROMAOTH, at the north end of the graveyard. This will attract the spirit. Now walk about the animal in the way of the Labyrinth, that is, in an unclosed circle from right to left, then return inside the first circle, the movement repeated thrice. The spirit will follow, and will become trapped in the Labyrinth until sunrise.

Place a gargoyle, fashioned in stone and stolen from a ruined church, close to the grave wherein lies the corpse to be summoned. At four points around the grave place small bronze bells, which have been rung at High Mass. The church, in whose night shadow the summoning will occur, should be surmounted by a weather cock. These three things discourage demons from following the spirit that will be called.

Editor's Note: John Dee lived from 1527 to 1608; he was a mathematician and astronomer, and one of the astrologers to Queen Elizabeth 1st. Fascinated by mysticism he joined forces, ten years after Rofomagus' death, with Edward Kelly, a supposed adept at clairvoyance and communion with Angels, and made a great study of spirits, angels and demons which he published as *A True and faithful relation of what passed for many years between Dr J. Dee and some spirits*. Kelly was the worst of the charlatans Dee encountered, and without talent, and his exposure badly damaged John Dee's only standing, and cast a shadow on his work, a slight which has been lifted in recent years.

Now prepare an unbroken circle around the grave, well marked with the body soil from the days of preparation. Ensure that no items of tin, copper, gold or iron are present. Ensure that all raiment worn by all in attendance are of black. Open the grave and take up the corpse, and lay it within the circle with its head turned to the east, and its limbs positioned as Christ was crucified. Inscribe, in dirt, inside the circle the names RAPHAEL, RAEL, MIRATON, TARMIEL, REX, SATURNUS. Others will give greater protection, but these are sufficient. In the bronze brazier burning henbane and the rest, now add mandrake, and strike at the flames with an ash staff. Strike the corpse three times with the staff. Now place a silver dish containing wine, mastic and sweet oil by the right hand of the body, and light it. Again strike the corpse thrice and command the spirit to return to the body with the words: 'May N. who is dust wake from sleep in the name of those who dwell in the Void, Persephone, Erehkigel, Thoth and Anubis, by the gods of the underworld and all the legions of the dead untimely snatched from life. In Hecate's name may he step out of his dust and answer to my demands, and by virtue of the Holy Resurection and the agonies of the damned. In the name of the Father I conjure and command thee, spirit of N. deceased, to answer to my demands and obey these sacred ceremonies on pain of everlasting torment. BERALD, BEOALD, BALBIN, GAB, GABOR, AAGABA, arise, arise, I charge and command thee.'

It will be necessary to assist the corpse upright. The voice will be faint and reedy, difficult to hear. It will answer questions briefly, truthfully, and for the best part of an hour. Beware: if the corpse is not burned with lime after use it will rise of its own accord and pursue the errant necromancer. The corpse of a suicide is ideal for consultation on matters of the future, for the spirit is tied to earth and remains so for many years, but is able to see clearly into the realm that is denied it. Strike such a corpse nine times nine with the staff. Beware especially of raising the corpse of a soldier, or any man who has died in battle, for they are protected by Mars, and the demon Asmodeus.

Rofomagus used such necromantic practice only infrequently, for it

...much weakens and maligns the spirit, and affects the will. The touch of Hell is felt even with the most stringent protection. It is a base and dangerous evocation, much to be avoided. If vigour and health are badly depleted it will be necessary to wear bracelets of tin, to wear blue, and to invoke BETHOR, THOR and TARANATH in each hour of Jupiter.

Three times Rofomagus summoned the dead. Each time he consulted them about the true Prince to summon if he was to control the very highest of the Lords of Darkness.

Each spirit, speaking through its stiffened flesh, has assured me that Marchosias is He who I should address for my final task.

Summoning Demon

Throughout Rofomagus's manuscripts are scattered references, usually quite cryptic, to the 'quest' which he saw himself as having embarked upon. The nature of this 'quest', as gradually becomes clear, was both simple and overwhelmingly ambitious: to find the knowledge which would enable him to both summon and bind to his will the supreme Princes of Hell, who may not normally be subject to any mortal's command.

That there is a clear hierarchy of demons is not widely understood, and their names are often used interchangeably in everyday parlance, even though this confuses several quite distinct beings. Supreme among them is Satan himself, also known as Lucifer. Next to him are three Princes of equal rank: Sathanas, Beelzebub and Put Satanachia (sometimes called Baphomet). Each of these commands two ministers, among whom is Lucifuge Rofocale. It is at this ministerial level that pacts are drawn.

By forcing Lucifuge Rofocale into a pact where he was obliged to obey without conditions, Carlyle had achieved something which no other magus in history claims to have matched. His pride in this, and in the name which it entitled him to take, is evident in the passage quoted at the beginning of Chapter 1. But this evidently was not enough. His last writings record an attempt to perform a still more audacious and improbable feat. In order to do this, he tells us, it was necessary to extract information from the demons themselves.

These last two years I have five times summoned and interrogated the great Marquis Marchosias, who was clearly indicated, both by my observation of Merlin and my experiments in necromancy, to be the Prince from whom the information I must have might be gained. Before Satan's fall he was a great Prince in Heaven, and he hopes yet to be restored to the Seventh Throne, though he must wait twelve hundred years for this. His virtue is that he speaks the truth, but the magus must nevertheless be cautious in acting upon the information thus obtained, for he is skilled in the sophistries of debate and will only provide the exact degree of truth required by a question; careless phraseology on the part of the operator will lead to him receiving dangerously inadequate answers.

The summoning of Marchosias requires no special skill, but before he could be forced into giving the information sought it was necessary to take steps to increase the power of the invocation. On the first four occasions my preparations were insufficient, and all my endeavours would not draw from him the answers I sought. At the fifth attempt I was successful. For this I had fumigated the instruments with an aspergillum of hyssop, basil, periwinkle, sage and vervain, a combination of herbs which I had observed used to powerful effect by the oracles. The sword of the art was freshly forged, and the steel quenched and tempered in a bath of pipistrelle's blood mixed with the juice of juniper berries.

Marchosias proved always a most reluctant demon to appear: I think this due to his knowledge of my line of inquiry. It was necessary for me to plunge my staff thrice into the brazier, intensifying my adjurations all the while, and finally invoke the Curse of the Chains, before he would come. Throughout these processes the air was filled with a sound like the howling of a thousand distant wolves, a noise which might easily have unnerved a less practised operator. When he came it was amidst a shroud of yellow fumes whose odour was that of scorching bones. He was, as the *Lemegeton* described, in the form of a wolf with gryphon's wings and a serpent's tail. He breathed flames which parted harmlessly around the circle, leaving me untouched. I adjured him to adopt human form, which he did, taking the likeness of a black-bearded prince whose crown shone like the midsummer sun.

At first he refused to answer my questions, standing silently and staring at me with eyes that evinced a truly demonic hatred. After several refusals I drew forth the Pentacle which I had fashioned of virgin gold formed that same day by transmuting iron. Holding it aloft so that he could read the powerful symbols inscribed upon it, I bade him once again reply to my questions. He shielded his eyes and, after a pause, agreed, saying, 'Ask your questions. I will answer.'

I demanded of him whether his answers would be truthful and without deceit; he said that as I knew well, he spoke only the truth. I asked if it was possible to summon and to bind the Great Prince whom I wish to control. He would not answer again, and it was necessary to hold the Pentacle aloft and recite a curse of terrible portent before he spoke, saying, 'If you speak the correct words of summoning, He will come.' I demanded to know if He might be controlled once summoned, at which Marchosias said, 'If it is done properly, He will be bound.'

I outlined to the demon the form of the operation I have devised, and a great shudder passed through him. I insisted he confirm to me its efficacy, and he said, 'The knowledge you hold is correct and sufficient.'

Further adjurations could draw no more from him than repetition of these phrases, and in time I dismissed him. After the ceremony was ended my exhaustion was such that I rested for ten days, during which time I was in a deep and dreamless sleep. When eventually I awoke and recovered my strength I began to prepare for the greatest endeavour of my life, or of any magus's life, the invocation and control of the Great Prince, the Sabbath Goat himself, Put Satanachia.

The Final Spell

Rofomagus was determined to attempt something which all authoritative writings on the black arts would tell us is impossible. Satan and the three Princes who rank just below him in the hierarchy of Hell may not be commanded by mortal men; if summoned, they will not appear. Rofomagus evidently thought otherwise, and the conversation he records with the demon Marchosias suggests that his belief was well-founded.

Why should he have believed this? There are various clues in his writings. It is clear that he thought his underground chamber to be a powerful locus of occult forces, a place in which magical operations would, because of its nature, tend to be more effective. He records having found on the wall an ancient carved representation of the seal of Lucifuge Rofocale. This carving was found during the excavation of the chamber, and by its side was a second seal, which does not match any recorded in occult texts but which has a design which, to Rofomagus at least, was suggestive of great power. Can this have been — or could he have believed it to be — the seal of Put Satanachia? From his journal, especially from his vision of Merlin, it is clear that Rofomagus believed the Neolithic people who had erected the mound, and the tomb within the mound, had summoned and controlled demons of major potency; this would account for the strange history of the site during the centuries that followed, a history that would indicate worship, or acknowledgement of some lingering power. It might also account for Ruckhurst's more recent history of haunting — did some residuum of the elemental force, summoned by the ancients, give rise to the Manor's reputation as one of the most haunted houses in England?

In the course of his researches Rofomagus investigated many different forms of magic, and found value in all. This too is of interest. Most scholars of the history of magic deal with the different traditions — Celtic magic, Egyptian magic, Greek magic, cabalistic magic etc — as though they were quite distinct, but this is a philosophical rather than a practical approach. It is clear that a practising magus would take useful knowledge from wherever he could find it.

There is only one journal entry following that describing the encounter with Marchosias. It is quite short, and perhaps reflects a lingering uncertainty in Rofomagus (an uncertainty which may *in itself* have worked towards his failure, since as his manuscript comments elsewhere belief is an important element in the success of any magical operation).

My preparations are complete, and at dawn I begin the purification of my body and of the instruments I shall use. Ten days from now I shall embark on the greatest and most perilous operation ever attempted by any magus. Fellow members of the Enneas, to whom I have confided my ambitions, counsel me against this step; they say I fall victim to that overweening pride the Greeks called *hubris*: the pride which comes before a fall. Yet I am confident of success.

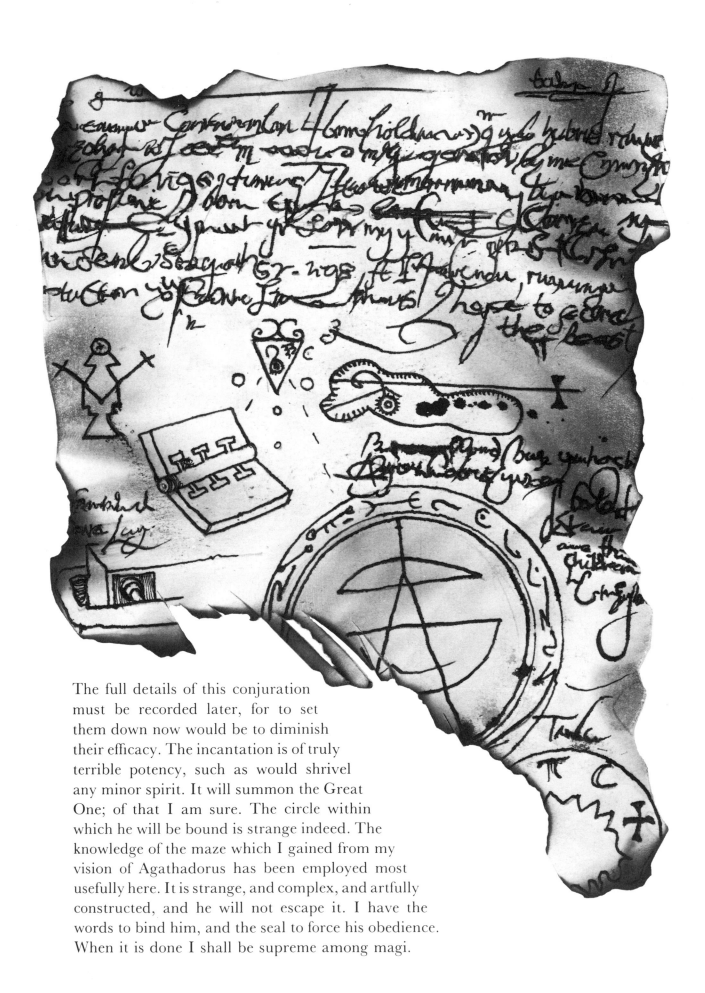

The full details of this conjuration must be recorded later, for to set them down now would be to diminish their efficacy. The incantation is of truly terrible potency, such as would shrivel any minor spirit. It will summon the Great One; of that I am sure. The circle within which he will be bound is strange indeed. The knowledge of the maze which I gained from my vision of Agathadorus has been employed most usefully here. It is strange, and complex, and artfully constructed, and he will not escape it. I have the words to bind him, and the seal to force his obedience. When it is done I shall be supreme among magi.

So ends Rotomagus's journal. We can only speculate as to what ensued, but from the physical evidence of his underground chamber it seems probable that he did succeed in summoning a supreme power, but was unable to control it. Analysis of the remains suggests that an extraordinarily intense heat was generated in the chamber, reaching as much as 400°C for a few seconds. In such a holocaust papers and even flesh would burst into flame; the manuscripts which survive, though scorched, do so because they were some distance from the heart of the conflagration, and being stored in a stone niche, beneath his workbench, were protected from the worst of the heat.

The prosaic explanation would be that he inadvertently compounded some explosive or combustible mixture and destroyed himself in that way. If this was accepted one could then dismiss the entire manuscript as the work of a self-deluding man. Sceptics will undoubtedly seize on this version of events. But is this likely? Carlyle was a learned man of his time, a scientist and alchemist as well as an occultist. He was unlikely to destroy himself in a silly laboratory accident. His manuscripts are detailed, consistent, and — where they match other extant authorities — authentic. Is it not more probable that he did achieve what he set out to achieve, even if he was destroyed at the moment of his triumph? We can readily visualise him as he completes his 'incantation of truly terrible potency', watching in awe and triumph as the great, shadowy figure of Put Satanachia, the Sabbath Goat, took form in the restraining circle; we can imagine his triumph turning to despair as his carefully designed restraints proved inadequate, and the Great Prince of Hell reached out beyond the circle that was to bind him — in the process unleashing a momentary blast of infernal heat — and snatched Rofomagus away and to Hell.

Where did he go wrong? It is impossible to tell from his manuscript, since he refrains from giving details of the crucial preparation. (If he was even slightly unsure of success this seems a sensible precaution to protect anyone who might try to imitate him.) The most likely explanation is simply that he got some detail of the operation — perhaps even a trivial one — wrong. As we have seen in his journals, success in true magic depends on absolute adherence to the details of ritual, even when these seem pointless; when summoning a spirit as all-powerful as Put Satanachia, this would be more important than ever. His interrogation of Marchosias is at best ambiguous: the demon admits Rofomagus's knowledge is 'correct and sufficient', but in the exchanges recorded he never stipulates that the way in which he has *arranged* that knowledge in the ritual is correct and sufficient. Even if the magus had all the right elements, but even in slightly the wrong order, it might have spelled his doom.

Study of the markings on the chamber's floor has produced interesting results. The circle in which the magus stood is of a familiar kind, though some-what modified. That in which the demon would appear is, however, most unusual, consisting of a strange spiralling pattern that must have been intended as a symbolic rendition of a maze from which he could not escape. Analysis of the charred remnants of braziers and candle-holders is expected to yield signi-ficant information on the details of the ritual, but in the absence of his grimoire itself it is likely to be a long time before any ambitious contemporary magician is in a position to follow in the footsteps of Geoffrey Carlyle, Rofomagus.

Index